REPORT NO. HAC-01-197-3P

PILOT'S HANDBOOK

FLIGHT OPERATING INSTRUCTIONS

For

XF-11 AIRPLANE

SERIAL NUMBER AAF 44-70156

(MFG. MODEL DESIGNATION D-5)

POWERED WITH PRATT & WHITNEY MODEL R-4360-37 ENGINES

(ENGINE MFG. & MODEL DESIGNATION A-7040)

MANUFACTURED BY HUGHES AIRCRAFT COMPANY

CONTRACT W33-038 ac-1079 SPEC. 01-2 Dated 1 December 1944

January 1947

Hughes XF-11 Pilot's Flight Operating Instructions
©2008-2009 Periscope Film LLC
All Rights Reserved
ISBN#978-1-935327-79-0   1-935327-79-8

REPORT NO. HAC-01-197-SP

RESTRICTED

PILOT'S HANDBOOK

FLIGHT OPERATING INSTRUCTIONS

For

XF-11 AIRPLANE

SERIAL NUMBER AAF 44-70156

(MFG. MODEL DESIGNATION D-5)

POWERED WITH PRATT & WHITNEY MODEL R-4360-37 ENGINES

(ENGINE MFG. & MODEL DESIGNATION A-7040)

MANUFACTURED BY HUGHES AIRCRAFT COMPANY

CONTRACT W33-038 ac-1079 SPEC. 01-2 Dated 1 December 1944

NOTICE: This document contains information affecting the National Defense of the United States within the meaning of the Espionage Act, 50 U. S. C., 31 and 32 as amended. Its transmission or the revelation of its contents in any manner to an unauthorized person is prohibited by law.

Approved by Chief, Eng. Div.   January 1947

RESTRICTED

1

TABLE OF CONTENTS

TABLE OF CONTENTS

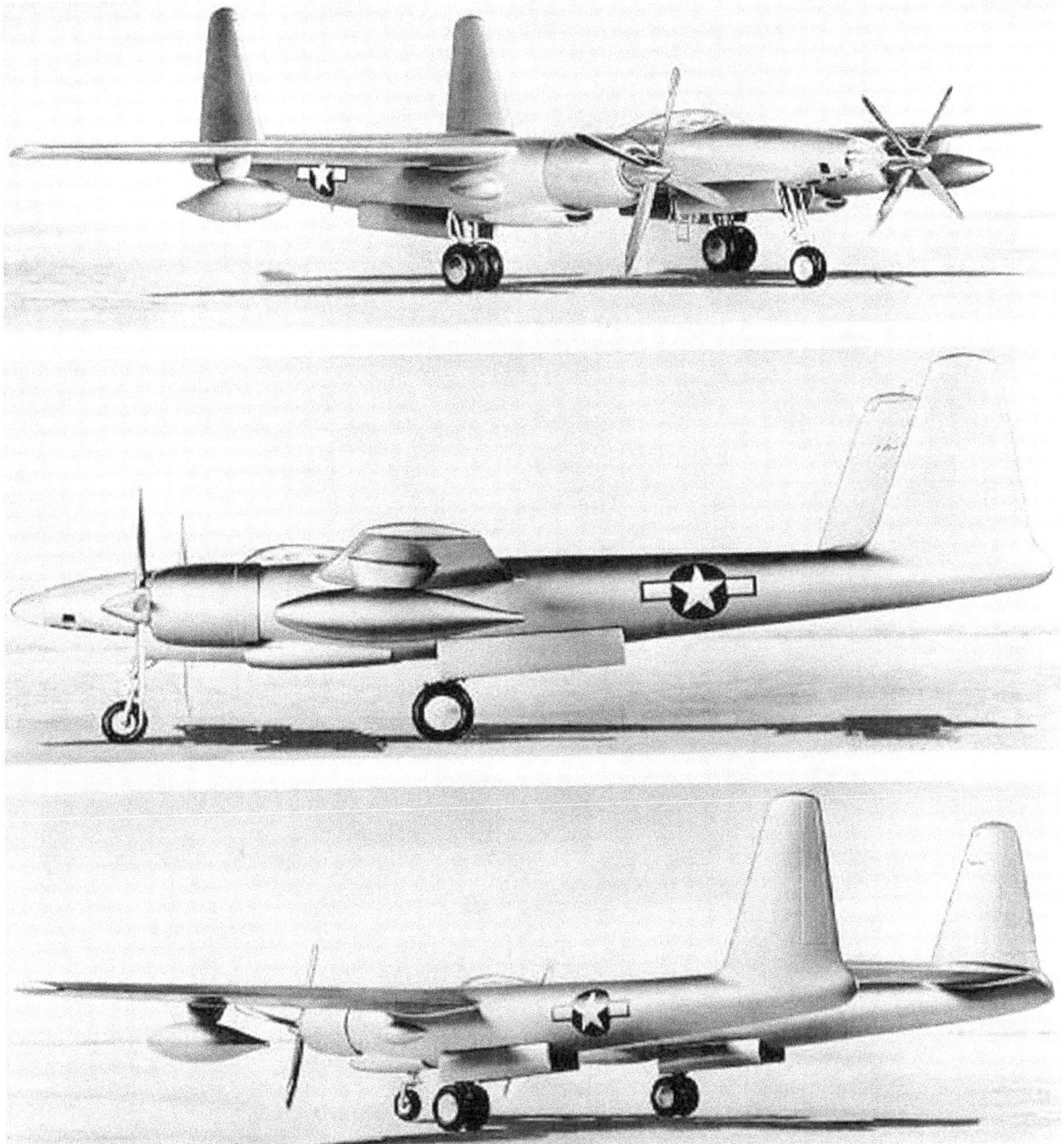

OVERALL DIMENSIONS
SPAN   101 FEET 4 INCHES
LENGTH 65 FEET 5 INCHES
HEIGHT 23 FEET 2 INCHES

Figure 1 - Three Views of Airplane.

SECTION I.

DESCRIPTION

1-1. GENERAL.

a. AIRPLANE.-The XF-11 is a two-engine photographic-reconnaissance airplane, pressurized for high altitude operation. The crew consists of a pilot and a navigator, the navigator performing the duties of the radio operator and photographer as well as relief pilot. The airplane has a wing span of 101 feet 4 inches, a length of 65 feet 5 inches, and a height of 23 feet 2 inches. The maximum recommended take-off gross weight is 60,000 pounds. See figure 10 for interior arrangement.

b. POWER PLANTS.-The airplane is powered by two Pratt & Whitney Model R-4360-37 radial air-cooled, 28 cylinder engines. Seven dual magnetos are mounted on each engine to furnish the ignition. An injection type carburetor, and two variable speed, centrifugal type air compressor turbosuperchargers are installed on each engine.

c. PROPELLERS.-Each engine is equipped with a Curtiss C644S-B, four bladed, electric propeller, with two-engine synchronizer control and boosted voltage feathering.

1-2. FLIGHT CONTROLS.

a. GENERAL.-The ailerons, elevators, and rudders are controlled in the conventional manner. Spoilers on each wing are mechanically interconnected with the ailerons and work automatically with aileron control.

b. TRIM TABS.-A toggle switch (19 figure 15) on the control pedestal switch panel controls the electrically operated aileron trim tab located on the left aileron only. The elevator trim tab is manually controlled by a wheel (11 figure 15) on the control pedestal. The rudder trim tabs are controlled electrically by a switch (20 figure 15) located on the pedestal switch panel. The aileron and rudder trim tab position indicator (26 figure 7) is located on the pilot's instrument panel. The elevator tab position indicator is located adjacent to the control wheel.

c. WING FLAPS.-The hydraulically operated wing flaps are controlled by a handle (12 figure 15) located on the side of the control pedestal. Position indicators of the flap control include selection of position in 10° increments from 0° (full up) to 40° (full down). Detents on the control quadrant are provided at the 0° and 40° positions, with a release push button incorporated

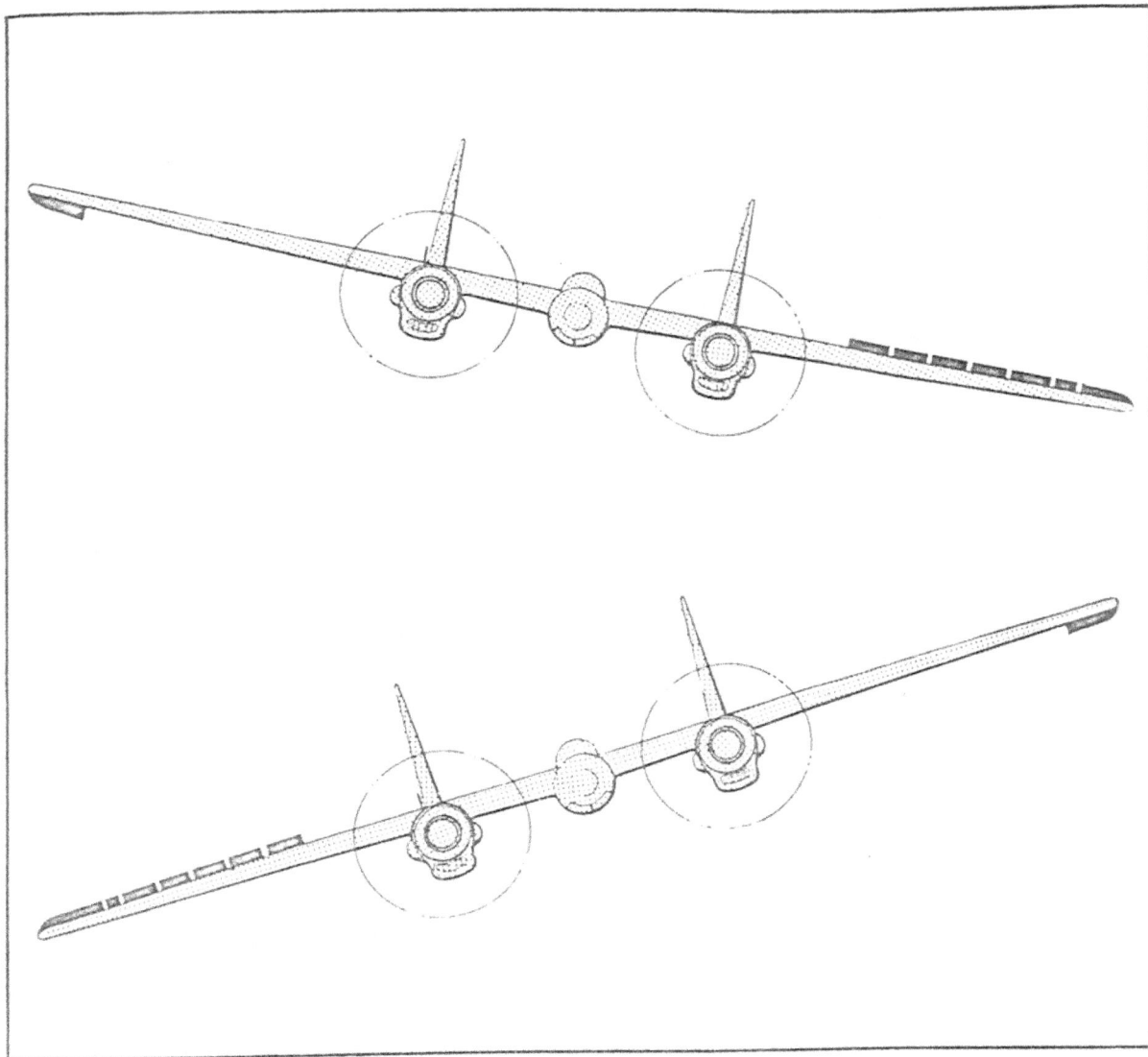

Figure 2 - Spoiler Operation.

in the handle. The flaps automatically stop at the selected position.

d. SURFACE CONTROL LOCK.-The surface control lock (figure 12) is manually operated and locks all flight control surfaces in neutral. When not in use the locking arm is stowed in a clip as shown in figure 12.

e. AUTOMATIC PILOT.-The major components comprising the Pioneer P-1 pilot are the master direction indicator (8 figure 7), gyro-horizon control indicator (10 figure 7), and a bank-and-turn indicator (6 figure 7). All are located on the pilot's instrument panel. These instruments are used as conventional instruments whenever the auto-pilot is disengaged. The controller unit (17 figure (17 figure 6), located on the pilot's right arm rest when in use, is stowed below the radio compass control box (11 figure 4) when not in use. The controller unit (17 figure 6) incorporates a turn control knob, a pitch trim vernier wheel, and a bank trim wheel. Operation of the power switch (figure 8) controls the automatic pilot gyros; the clutch button (figure 8) engages or disengages the servo units. In emergencies the automatic pilot servo units can be mechanically disengaged by pushing down the servo disconnect handle (11 figure 5). Re-engagement of the servo units cannot be made in flight.

1-3. LANDING GEAR CONTROLS

a. NORMAL.-The handle (12 figure 6) on the lower control pedestal controls the hydraulically operated landing gear. A lock release lever is incorporated in the landing gear handle knob. A warning horn and two position lights (25 figure 7) on the pilot's instrument panel are provided to indicate gear position. The horn operates when the gear is not locked down or the nose wheel is not turned to the proper position while either throttle is retarded. The warning horn shut-off push-button switch (5 figure 15) is located on the control pedestal switch panel.

b. EMERGENCY.-There is no emergency mechanical system for lowering the gear. The gear may be operated on the emergency hydraulic system by moving the handle to down position and placing the emergency hydraulic switch (figure 8) to "ON".

1-4. BRAKE CONTROLS.

a. GENERAL.-Conventional toe-pedal brakes are provided. The parking brake handle (29 figure 7) is located on the pilot's instrument sub-panel.

b. EMERGENCY BRAKE.-The emergency brake system is operated by a lever (20 figure 6) located on the floor to the right of the pilot's seat and obtains hydraulic pressure from the emergency

PILOT'S COMPARTMENT - FORWARD

Key to Figure 3.

1. Control Pedestal
2. Fluorescent Light
3. Pilot's Oxygen Regulator
4. L. H Windshield Defroster
5. Pilot's Clear View Panel
6. Landing Gear Warning Placard
7. Remote Compass Correction Card
8. Fire Detector Test Switch
9. Inverter Indicator Light
10. Camera "ON" Warning Light
11. Engine Fire Warning Lights
12. Pilot's Instrument Panel
13. APS-13 Signal Indicator Light
14. R. H. Windshield Defroster
15. Cabin Heater Outlet Diffuser
16. Torque Indicator
17. (Deleted)
18. Airplane Check List
19. First Aid Kit
20. Fluorescent Light
21. Inter-Aircraft Signal Light
22. CO_2 Fire Extinguisher
23. Thermos Bottles
24. Cabin Pressure Regulator
25. Auto Pilot Check List
26. Pilot's Test Instrument Panel
27. Control Surface Lock

Figure 3 - Pilot's Compartment - Forward.

PILOT'S COMPARTMENT - RIGHT SIDE

Key to Figure 4.

1. CO_2 Fire Extinguisher

2.   Fluorescent Light

3.   Inter-Aircraft Signal Light

4.   Inter-Aircraft Signal Light Filters

5.   Recognition Light Control Panel

6   Cabin Air Instrument Panel

7.   Cabin Air Control Panel

8.   Radio Control Panel

9.   Flash Light

10.   Radio Compass Control Box

11.   Auto Pilot Controller (Stowed)

12.   Navigator's Radio Jack Box

12A. Cord Assembly

13.   Navigator's Oxygen Panel

14.   Navigator's Oxygen Regulator

15.   Pyrotechnic Pistol Mount

16.   Pyrotechnic Pistol Holder and Cartridge Case

17.   Sense Antenna

18.   Thermos Bottles

19.   Hand Axe

20.   Cabin Pressure Warning Signal

21.   Auto Pilot Amplifier Adapter

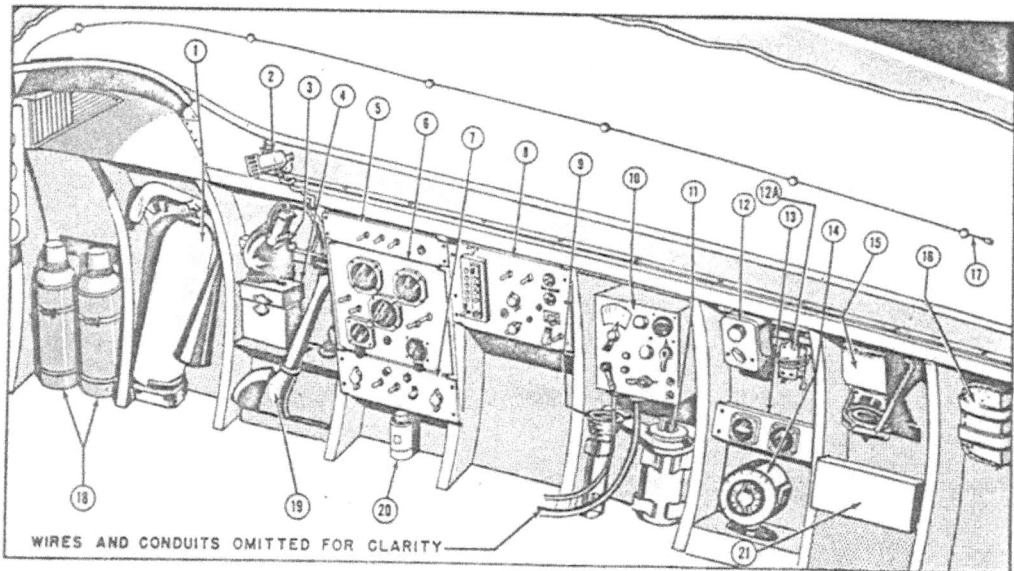

WIRES AND CONDUITS OMITTED FOR CLARITY

Figure 4 - Pilot's Compartment - Right Side.

hydraulic system. The lever is pulled up to apply the brakes and
turned right or left for differential control. Emergency hydraulic
system pump switch (figure 8) must be in "ON" position to operate
emergency brakes.

1-5. HYDRAULIC SYSTEM.

a. NORMAL SYSTEM.-The normal hydraulic system operates the
landing gear, wing flaps, and brakes. Hydraulic pressure is obtained from two engine-driven pumps (one on each engine), supplying
hydraulic fluid under 1250 to 1500 psi pressure. The hydraulic
system pressure gage (35 figure 7) is located on the pilot's instrument sub-panel.

b. EMERGENCY HYDRAULIC SYSTEM.-An emergency electric-driven
hydraulic pump, operated by switch (figure 8) on the pilot's left
switch panel, supplies pressure for the emergency hydraulic system.
Separate lines are utilized for operating the landing gear and
brakes.

1-6. ELECTRICAL SYSTEM.

a. GENERAL.-The electrical system consists of a generator on
each engine, a 24 volt battery located in the aft fuselage fairing,
a main and a standby three phase inverter, and a main and a standby
single phase inverter. The two guarded generator switches are
located at the bottom of the pilot's left switch panel. (See
figure 8.

b. CIRCUIT BREAKERS.-Individual circuits are protected by
circuit breakers located in the main junction box. A master re-set
push button, located on the pilot's instrument sub-panel (30 figure
7), will close all but the four propeller circuit control circuit
breakers that may be open. The propeller control circuit breakers
push buttons (37 figure 7) are located on the pilot's instrument
sub-panel.

c. IGNITION AND BATTERY SWITCHES.-A combination master battery
and ignition switch is located on the pilot's left switch panel,
with the following positions: "IGN OFF BATT OFF", "IGN ON BATT ON",
and "IGN ON". Two individual engine ignition switches are located
at the top of the pilot's left switch panel. (See figure 8.) The
master battery and ignition switch must be moved to the "IGN ON
BATT ON" position before the individual ignition switches can be
operated. The "IGN ON" position is for emergency operation only.
In this position the ignition to both engines is "ON" despite the
position of the individual ignition switches and the entire
electrical system is "OFF".

d. INVERTERS.-Alternating current is supplied by a main and
standby single phase inverter and a main and standby three phase

PILOT'S COMPARTMENT - AFT

Key to Figure 5.

1. Pyrotechnic Pistol Installation

2. Radio Compass Sense Antenna

3. Aft Canopy Emergency Release

4. Upper Movable Armor Plate (Down Position)

5. Upper Movable Armor Plate (Up Position)

6. Movable Armor Plate Lock

7. Astro Compass

8. Navigator's Spot Light

9. Navigator's Fluorescent Light

10. Dinghy Radio

11. Auto-Pilot Emergency Servo Disconnect Handle

12. Pilot's Switch Panel Spot Light

12A. Astro Compass Case

13. Fixed Armor Plate

14. Navigator's Seat

15. Navigator's Shoulder Harness Inertia Lock and Take-up Reel

16. Navigator's Shoulder Harness

17. Navigator's Seat Adjusting Lever

18. Navigator's Heated Clothing Rheostat

19. Take-up Reel Control

20. Auto Pilot Amplifier Adapter

21. Map and Data Case

22. Disposal Cups

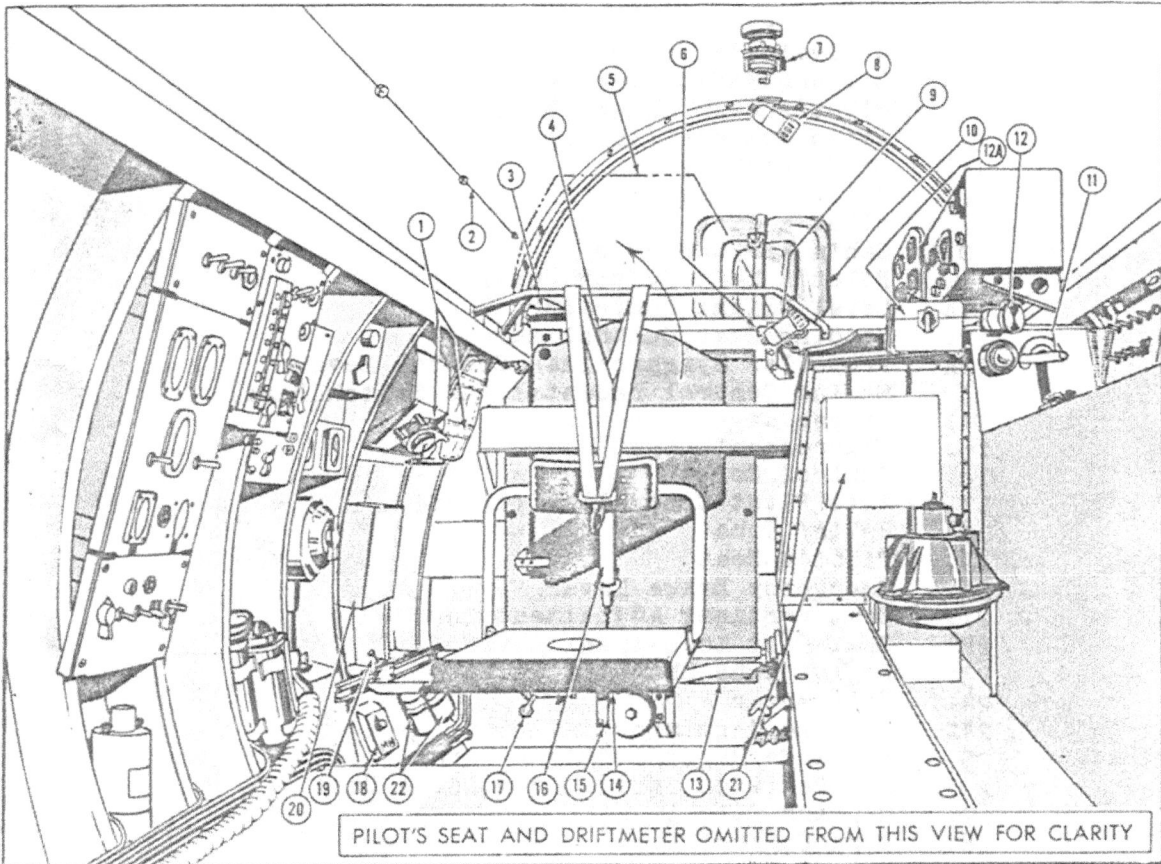

Figure 5 - Pilot's Compartment - Aft.

PILOT'S COMPARTMENT - LEFT SIDE

Key to Figure 6.

1.   Life Rafts (2)
1A.   Monitoring Switch
2.   Navigator's Table
3.   Radio Key
4.   Navigator's Instrument Panel
5.   Liaison Radio Receiver
6.   Pilot's Rear Armor Plate
7.   Astro Compass (In Use)
7A.   Driftmeter Switch
8.   Pilot's Filter Box
9.   Pilot's Jack Box
10.   Cabin Air Controls
11.   Pilot's Left Switch Panel
11A. Level Flight Indicator
12.   Landing Gear Control Handle
12A. Propeller Synchronizer Control Lever
13.   Engine Control Pedestal and Switch Panel
14.   Oxygen Regulator
15.   Fluorescent Light
16.   Control Column
17.   Auto Pilot Controller (In use)
18.   Relief Tube
19.   Pilot's Seat
20.   Emergency Brake Lever
21.   Seat Vertical Adjustment Lever
22.   Seat Tilt Adjustment Lever
23.   Relief Tube Shut-off Valve
24.   Driftmeter
24A. Voltage Regulator
25.   Entrance Hatch Jettison Lever
26.   Air Position Indicator Mileage Unit
27.   Map and Data Case
28.   Turn Control Knob
29.   Bank Trim Wheel
30.   Pitch Trim Vernier Wheel

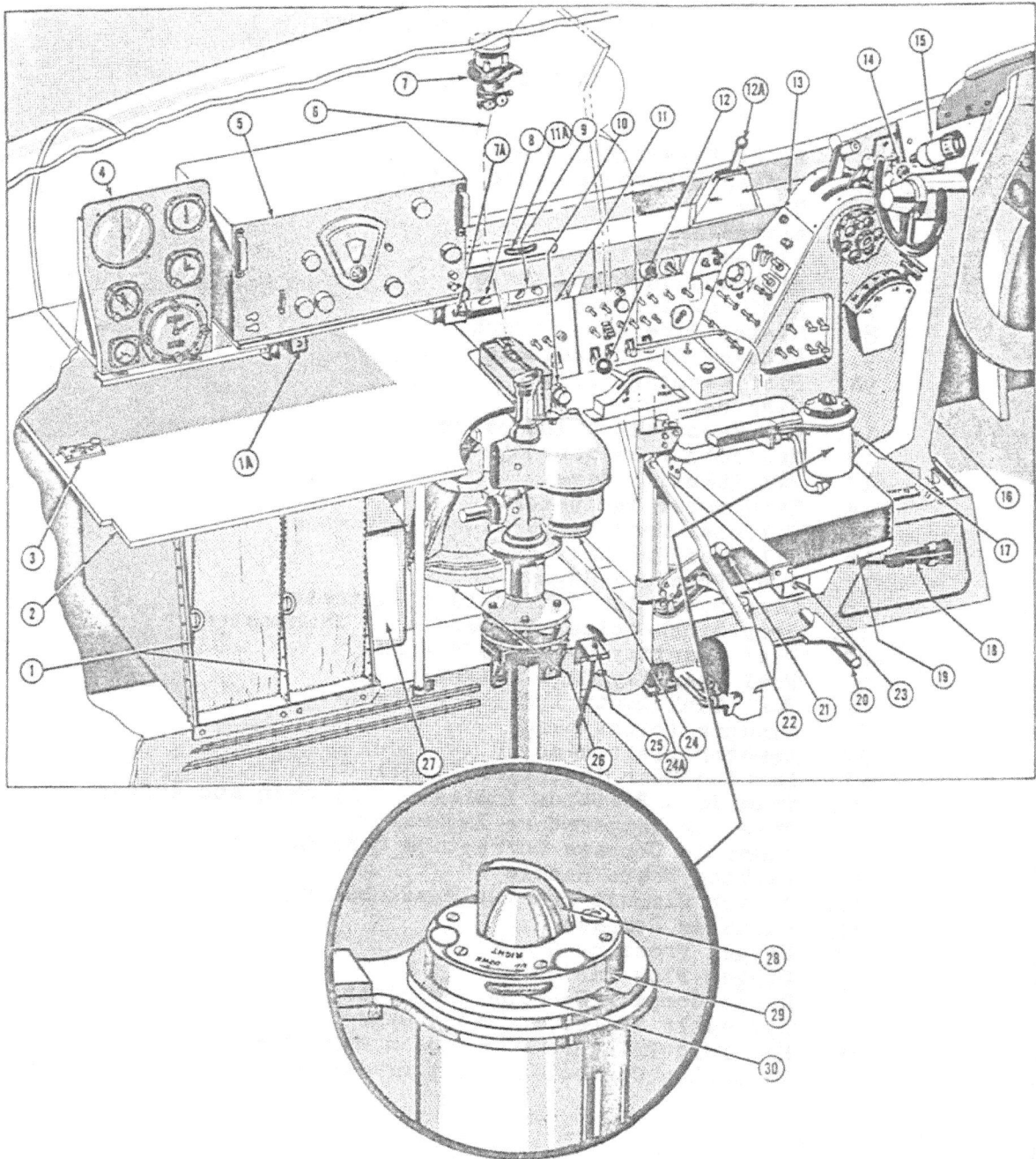

Figure 6 - Pilot's Compartment - Left Side.

PILOT'S INSTRUMENT PANEL

Key to Figure 7.

1. Pilot Director Indicator.
2. Marker Beacon Indicator Light.
3. Clock
4. Altimeter
5. Airspeed Indicator
6. Bank-and-Turn Indicator
7. Radio Call Plate
8. Master Direction Indicator
9. Rate-of-Climb Indicator
9A. Flap Warning Placard
10. Gyro Horizon
11. Oil Temperature Indicator
12. Manifold Pressure Gage
13. Oil Quantity Gage
14. Tachometer Indicator
15. Cylinder Head Temperature Indicator
16. Oil Pressure Gage
17. Fuel Pressure Gage
18. Carburetor Air Temperature Indicator
19. Prop Synchronizer Master Motor Tachometer
20. Fuel Quantity Gage (left-wing)
21. Fuel Quantity Gage (right-wing)
22. Fuel Tank Empty Indicator Lights.
23. Ammeter (right-hand)
24. Ammeter (left-hand)
25. Landing Gear Indicator Lights
26. Trim Tabs Position Indicator (Aileron and Rudder)
27. Free Air Temperature Indicator
28. Magnetic Compass Correction Card Holder
29. Parking Brake Handle
30. Master Circuit Breaker Reset Button
31. Magnetic Compass
32. Oxygen Pressure Gage
33. Oxygen Flow Indicator
34. Radio Compass Bearing Indicator
35. Hydraulic System Pressure Gage
36. Manifold Pressure Gage Drain Controls
37. Propeller Control Circuit Breakers

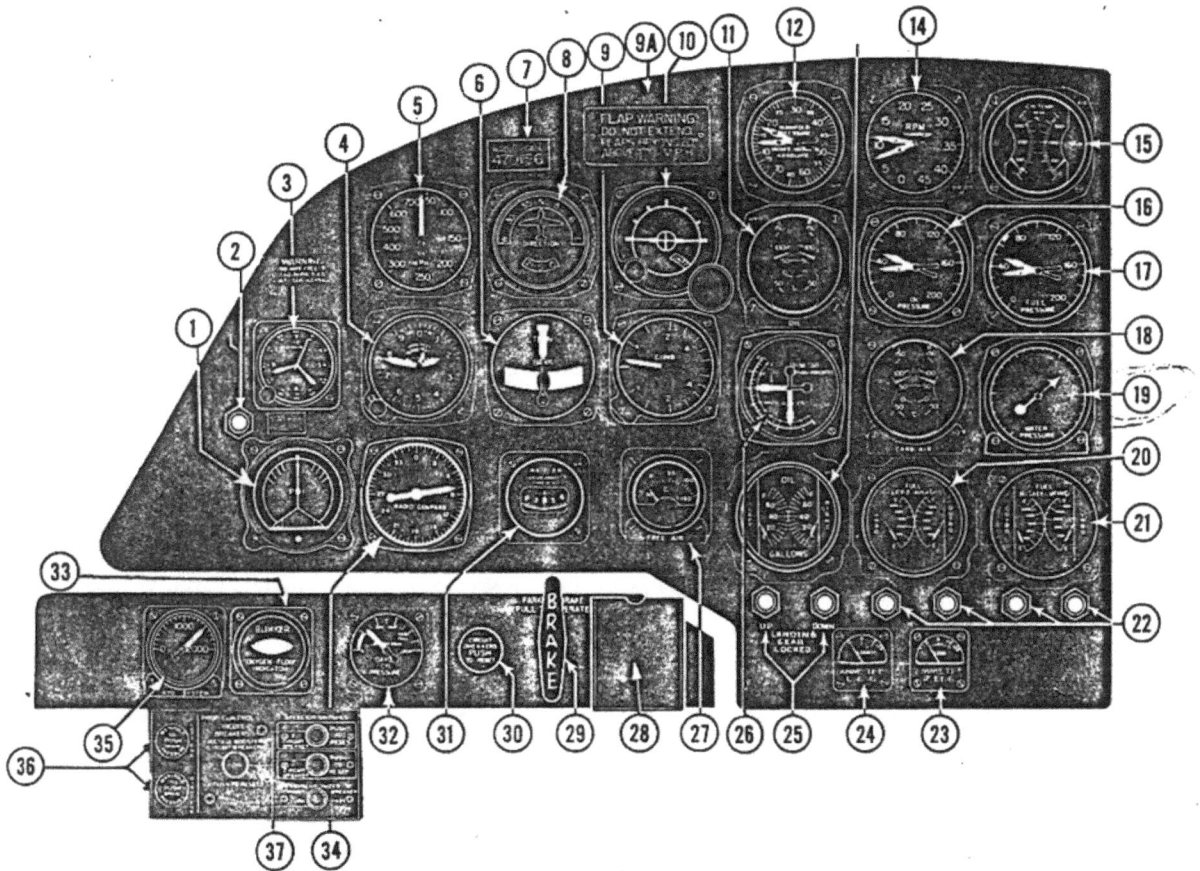

Figure 7 - Pilot's Instrument Panel.

inverter, with the switches located on the pilot's left switch panel. (See figure 8).

(1) The single phase inverter supplies power for the radio and the following equipment: turbo regulator and driftmeter.

(2) The three phase inverter supplies power to the automatic pilot and the air position indicator.

(3) If the main single phase inverter fails, the inverter change-over relay automatically starts the spare inverter, and the indicator light at the top of the switch panel (figure 8) comes on. If the spare inverter also fails the light on the instrument light shield (9 figure 3) will come on and manifold pressure must be adjusted with the throttles as stated on the placard located on the instrument light shield.

If the main three phase inverter (inverter No. 1) fails, pull out on the autopilot clutch switch to disengage the autopilot servos, leaving only the autopilot flight instruments operating, and move the toggle switch down to the "inverter No. 2" position.

e. LIGHTS

(1) PILOT'S COMPARTMENT LAMPS. (See figures 3, 4, and 5.)

(2) NAVIGATOR'S COMPARTMENT LAMPS. (See figure 5.)

(3) PHOTOGRAPHER'S COMPARTMENT LAMP. (See figure 3.)

(4) LANDING LIGHT SWITCH. (See figure 15.)

(5) POSITION LIGHT SWITCH. (See figure 15.)

(6) LANDING LIGHTS RETRACTING SWITCHES. (See figure 15.)

(7) RECOGNITION LIGHTS SWITCHES. (See figure 13.)

1-7. FUEL SYSTEM. (See figure 11.)

a. GENERAL.-Fuel is carried in two inboard and two outboard fuel tank groups and two drop tanks. The tank cross-feed and selector switches (figure 8) are located on the pilot's left switch panel. Fuel is transferred from the drop tanks to the outboard wing tanks only. Fuel shut-off valves are provided for each system. The tank usable fuel capacities are as follows:

```
Left outboard .... ... . . ... ..... 500 U. S. gallons
Left inboard ....... . . .. ... ... 490 U. S. gallons
Right inboard ............. . ... ... 615 U. S. gallons
Right outboard ................... ........500 U. S. gallons
                           Total 2105 U. S. gallons
```

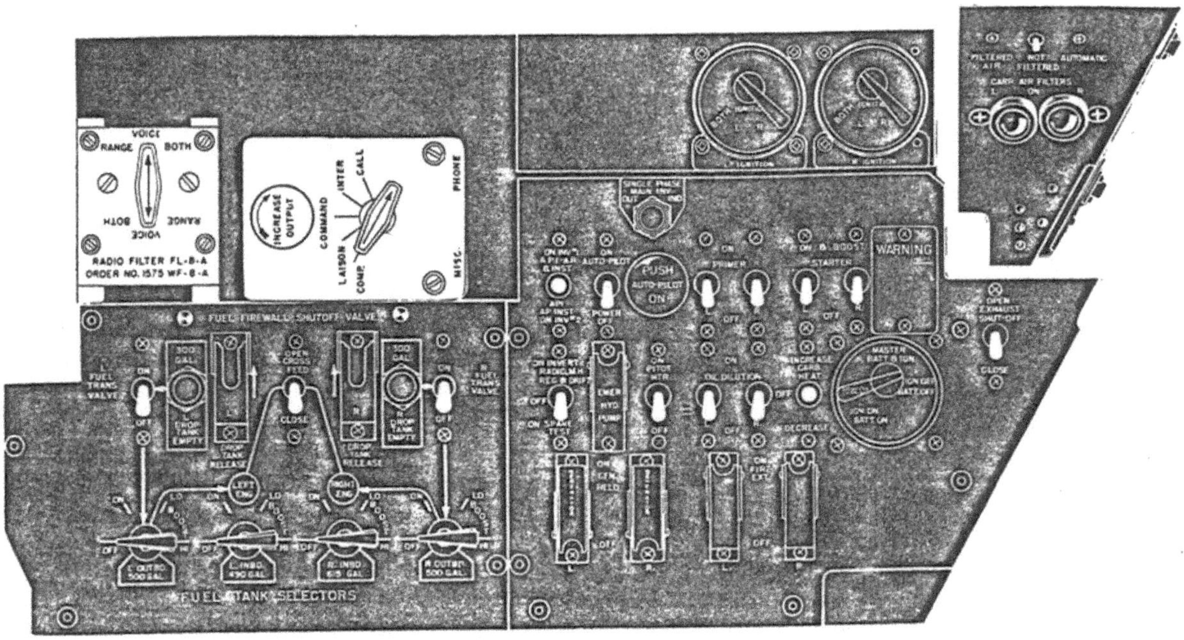

Figure 8 - Pilot's Left Switch Panel.

                            Total..... 2105 U. S. gallons
Drop tanks (300 gallons each)............. 600 U. S. gallons
                      Maximum Total..... 2705 U. S. gallons

b. FUEL BOOSTER AND SELECTOR SWITCHES.-The fuel tank selector switches, "LEFT INBOARD", "RIGHT INBOARD", "LEFT OUTBOARD", and "RIGHT OUTBOARD" indicate the four groups of wing fuel tanks from which fuel is to be drawn, with each switch having four positions, "OFF", "ON", "LO BOOST", and "HI BOOST". The "ON" position opens the tank selector valve and the "LO BOOST" and "HI BOOST" give the required fuel pressure. All tanks in each selected group are drained simultaneously.

c. CROSS-FEED.-The cross-feed switches and fuel tank switches, as shown in figures 8 and 18, operate the cross-feed system. Automatic check valves are provided for single engine operation.

d. TRANSFER SWITCHES.-The fuel transfer switches (figure 8) control the pumps which force the fuel from the drop tanks into the outboard wing tanks. Fuel cannot be otherwise transferred from one group of tanks into another. Indicator lights adjacent to the drop tank switches show when the drop tanks are empty.

e. DROP TANK RELEASE SWITCHES.-Two guarded switches, one beside each of the empty endicator lights on the pilot's left switch panel (figure 8) will release the drop tanks when empty.

f. FUEL FIREWALL SHUT-OFF VALVE SWITCHES.-A fuel firewall shut-off valve is installed in both fuel supply lines aft of the right and left firewalls. The fuel firewall shut-off valve switches (17 figure 15) are marked "OPEN" and "CLOSE" and are located on the control pedestal and switch panel. These switches must not be moved to "CLOSE" during operations except for emergencies.

g. ENGINE PRIMERS.-Two spring loaded switches (figure 8) operate the electric primers on the engines.

1-8. AIR INDUCTION SYSTEM. (See figure 9.)

a. GENERAL.-Ram air is taken through the air intake scoop and distributed through ducting to the oil coolers, the turbosuperchargers, the intercooler, and the carburetor. The induction system offers three selections of air: compressed air from the turbosuperchargers, filtered air through the filter door, and heated air when icing conditions prevail. Switches governing the various conditions are the intercooler air outlet switch, carburetor air heat switch, and carburetor air filter switch.

b. INTERCOOLER AIR OUTLET.-The carburetor air temperature during the operation of the turbosuperchargers is regulated by the intercooler air outlet switch (16 figure 15) located on the pilot's

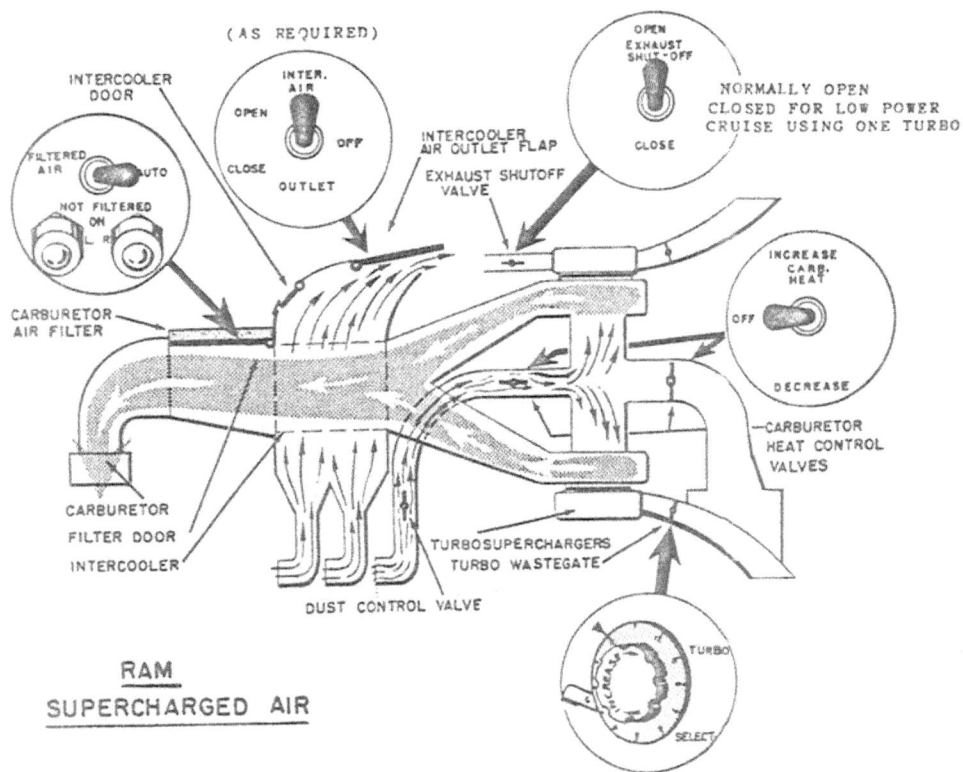

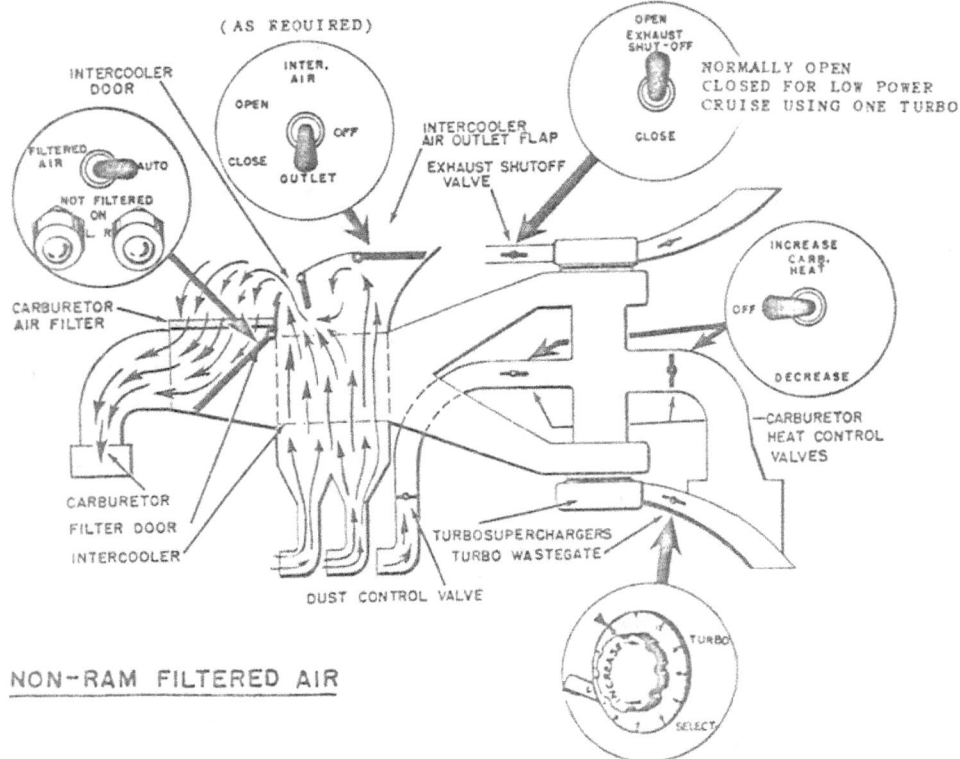

Figure 9 (Sheet 1 of 2) Air Induction System.

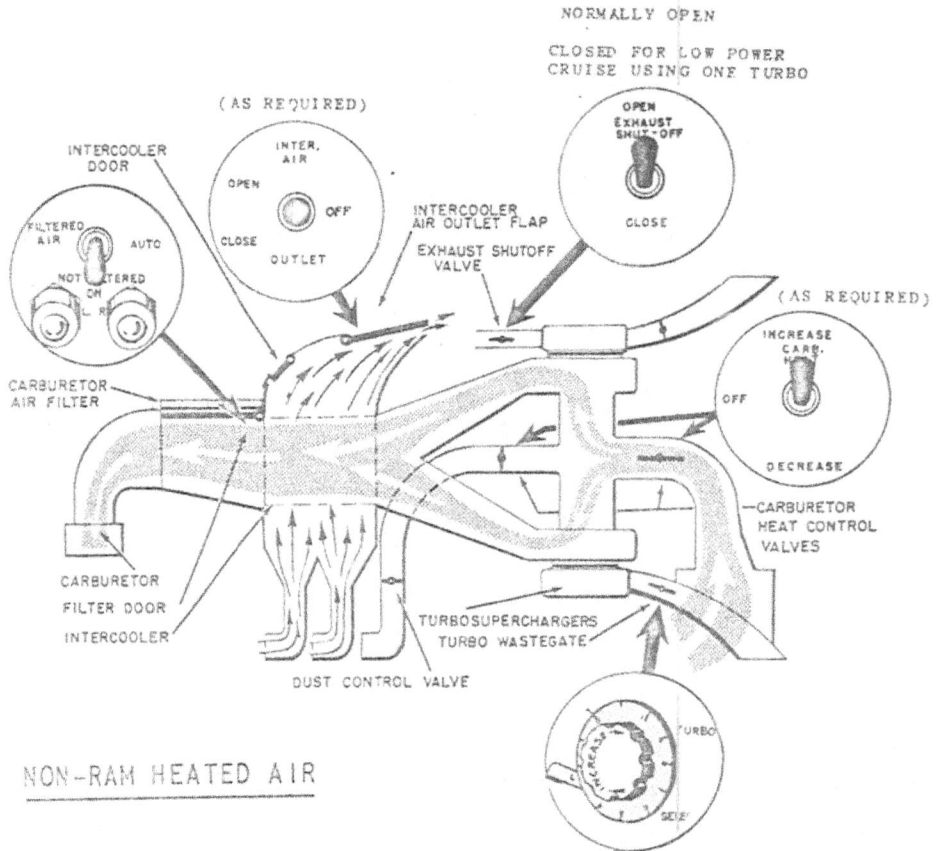

NON-RAM HEATED AIR

Figure 9 (Sheet 2 of 2) Air Induction System.

control pedestal. This switch opens or closes the intercooler air outlet flap (figure 9) as desired to obtain the proper carburetor air temperature while in flight. For ground runs and take-off without turbo boost, or whenever filtered air is used, the intercooler air outlet flap should be closed as air will then be drawn from the intercooler air outlet duct (figure 9) through the intercooler door and air filter into the carburetor.

c. CARBURETOR AIR FILTER.-The air filter door is operated automatically or manually by a switch (figure 8) on the pilot's left switch panel. All normal operations should be with the switch in the "AUTOMATIC" position. In this position there is a mechanical-electrical hook-up which opens the air filter door when the turbosupercharger waste gates are open. When the turbosuperchargers are operating (waste gates closed to some degree) the filter door (figure 9) and the door in the intercooler air outlet duct will automatically close. The "FILTERED AIR" and "NOT FILTERED AIR" positions should be used as an emergency manual override to provide control of the air filter valve in case of failure of the automatic system and the "NOT FILTERED AIR" position is used when carburetor heat is required when "FILTERED AIR" warning lights are on. The time required to fully open or close the carburetor air filter door is 17 seconds, with warning lights on the pilot's switch panel lighting up when in the "ON" position (filter doors open).

WARNING

When filtered air is desired for take-off from elevated fields, set turbo boost control at "0" before take-off.

NOTE

See paragraph 1-8, d, for air filter switch position with carburetor heat applied.

d. CARBURETOR AIR HEAT.-The "CARBURETOR HEAT" springloaded switch is located on the pilot's switch panel (figure 8). There are three positions of the switch: "INCREASE", "DECREASE", and "OFF". The hot air is taken from the shroud around the turbosupercharger and mixed with non-supercharged air ahead of the turbosupercharger. For controlling carburetor air heat, when turbo boost is being used, close intercooler air outlet flap as necessary.

WARNING

Filtered air cannot be used when carburetor heat is necessary. Therefore, if it is necessary to use carburetor head when filtered air warning lights are "ON", move the carburetor air filter switch to "NOT FILTERED".

RESTRICTED

When the necessity for carburetor hot air is past, hold carburetor
heat switch to "DECREASE" until carburetor heat control valve is
completely closed, then return carburetor air filter switch to
"AUTOMATIC" and carburetor heat switch to "OFF". Time to operate
valve from "INCREASE to "DECREASE" is approximately 12 seconds.

e. TURBOSUPERCHARGER SYSTEM.-The turbosupercharger system is
used to supply air for the air induction system and for pressuriza-
tion of the fuselage. An exhaust shut-off switch switch (figure 8)
located on the main switch panel is provided for low power cruising
with one turbosupercharger operating for each engine by placing the
switch to the "CLOSE" position.

f. TURBOSUPERCHARGER, MINNEAPOLIS HONEYWELL REGULATOR.-The
turbosupercharger control system is wired directly to the single
phase inverter, and is automatically energized when either inverter
is running. The boost selector dial unit (3 figure 15), located on
the control pedestal switch panel, regulates the manifold pressure
and the turbosupercharger speed. The dial is marked in increments
from "0" to "10". When the dial is placed at "0" the turbosuperchargers are off. For take-off the dial is placed at "8", except
as noted in "WARNING" in paragraph 8, c preceding.

NOTE

In case of high field altitude or high air
temperatures, where take-off power, RPM, and
manifold pressure cannot be obtained by ad-
vancing throttle with propellers in increase
RPM within maximum RPM limits of engine, increase boost until correct manifold pressure
is obtained. Filtered air cannot be used
with this condition.

1-9. OIL SYSTEM CONTROLS.

a. GENERAL.-Each engine receives its oil supply from a 70 U.S.
(58.3 Imp.) gallon, self-sealing tank. The oil cooler flaps are
either automatically controlled by a thermostatic temperature
control unit or manually controlled by switches on the pilot's
pedestal switch panel. (See figure 15.) The following positions
are indicated on each switch: "AUTOMATIC", "CLOSE", "OPEN", and
"OFF". The "OPEN" and "CLOSE" positions are spring loaded. The
time required for the oil cooler flaps to move from full open to
full close is 28 seconds.

b. OIL DILUTION SYSTEM.-The oil dilution switches (figure 8)
are located on the pilot's switch panel.

c. FIREWALL OIL SHUT-OFF VALVE SWITCHES.-The firewall oil
shutoff valves, for emergency use only, are controlled by switches
(18 figure 15) on the pilot's control pedestal.

FUSELAGE INTERIOR ARRANGEMENT DIAGRAM

Key to Figure 10.

1. Navigator's Seat

2. Navigator's Fixed Table

3. Driftmeter

3A. Navigator's Removable Table (Stowed)

4. Pilot's Seat

5. Engine Control Pedestal

6. Wheel and Control Column

7. Pilot's Instrument Panel

8. Navigator's Instrument Case

9. External Power Receptacle

10. Life Rafts

11. Map and Data Case

12. Fuel Filler

13. Oil Tank Filler Neck

14. Hydraulic Tank Filler

15. Oxygen Filler Valve

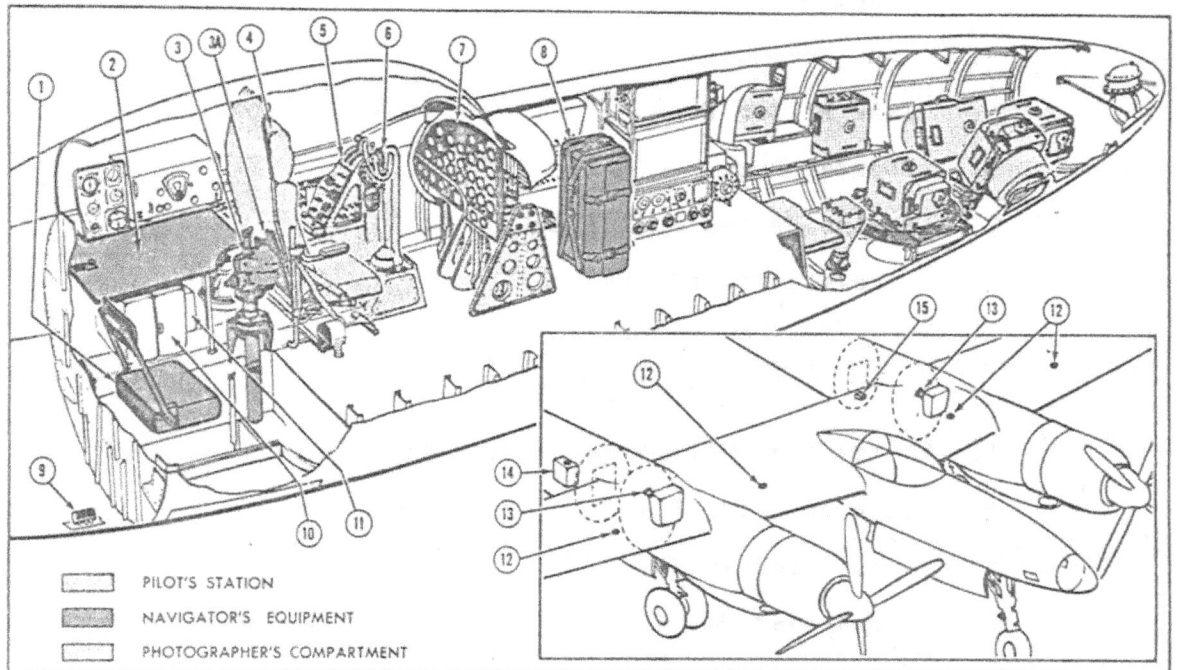

Figure 10 - Fuselage Interior.

PILOT'S STATION

NAVIGATOR'S EQUIPMENT

PHOTOGRAPHER'S COMPARTMENT

FUEL SYSTEM DIAGRAM

Key to Figure 11.

1.   Pressure Relief Valve

2.   Electric Motor Driven Air Pump

3.   Inlet Filter

4.   Tank Fuel Gage

5.   Tank Filler Neck

6.   Booster Pump

7.   Engine Driven Fuel Pump

8.   Firewall Shutoff Valve

9.   Tank Flapper Valve

10. Drop Tank-Empty Light Switch

11. Automatic Fuel Level Controller

12. Tank Selector Valve

13. Fuel Check Valve

14. Cross-Feed Valve

15. Fuel Strainer

MAIN LINES
VAPOR RETURN LINES
CROSS FEED LINE
FUEL PUMP BALANCE LINES

PRIMER LINES
PRIMER SOLENOID
CARBURETOR
AIR INTAKE

TANK CAPACITIES (NET)
LEFT AND RIGHT OUTBOARD TANKS —— 500 U.S. GALS.
LEFT INBOARD TANKS ————————— 490 "   "
RIGHT INBOARD TANKS ———————— 615 "   "
DROP TANKS ———————————————— 600 "   "

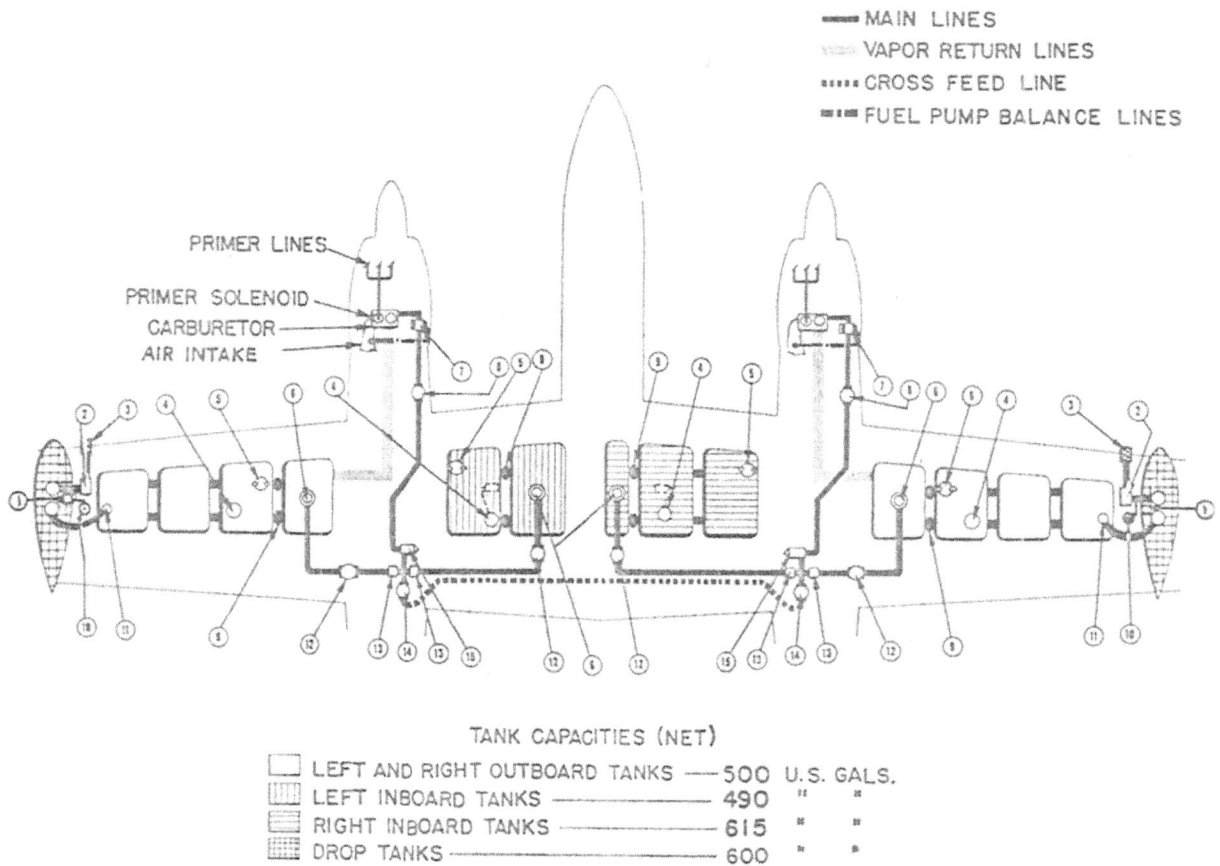

Figure 11 - Fuel System Diagram.

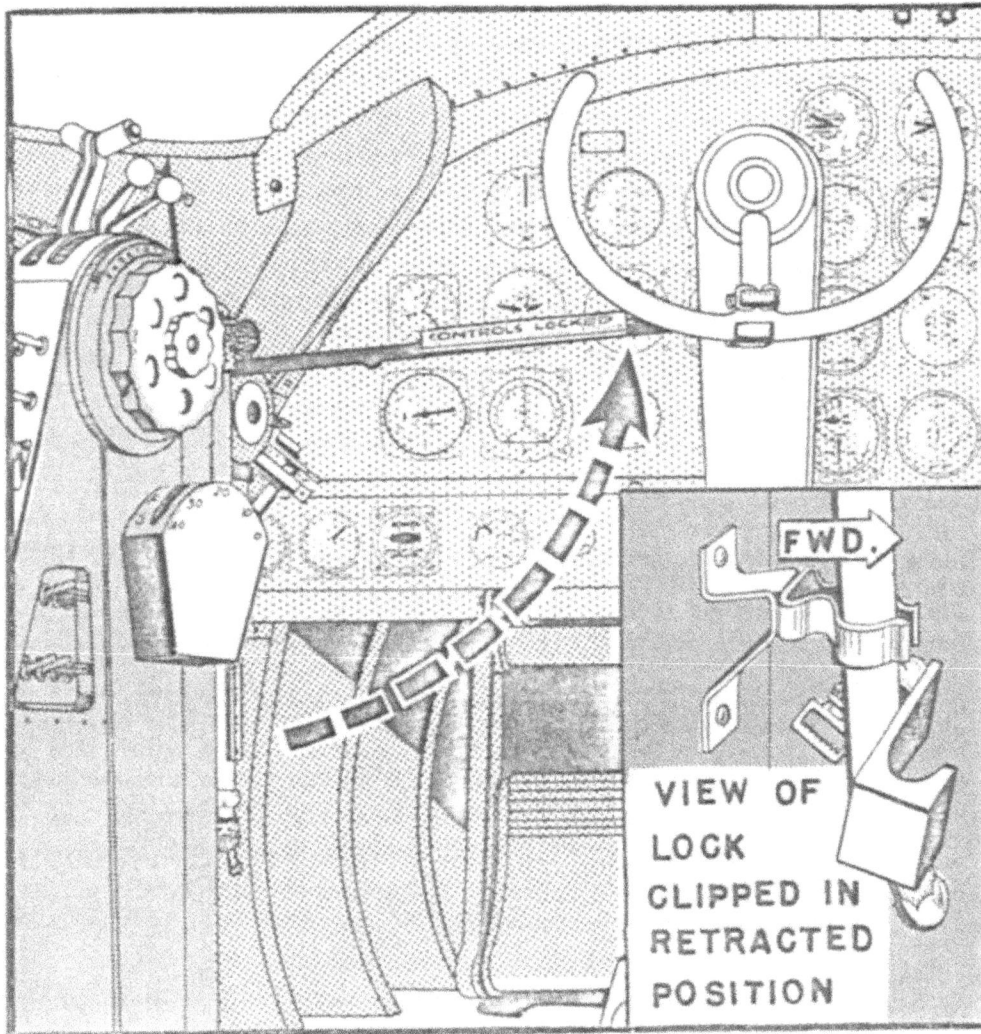

Figure 12 - Flight Surface Control Lock.

1-10. ENGINE CONTROLS.

    a. THROTTLE CONTROLS.-The throttle controls (8 figure 15) include the "OPEN" and "CLOSE" positions. The pilot's microphone switch is located on the right-hand throttle control.

    b. MIXTURE CONTROLS.-The mixture controls (10 figure 15) have markings for "AUTO-RICH", "AUTO-LEAN" and "IDLE CUT-OFF" positions.

    c. FRICTION LOCK.-The engine controls friction lock (21 figure 15) is located on the right-hand side of the control pedestal.

1-11. PROPELLER CONTROLS.

    a. GENERAL.-The propellers are electrically operated and controlled by two selector switches, a synchronizer control lever, and two propeller feathering switches. A master synchronizer motor tachometer and four circuit breakers are included in the system.

    b. PROPELLER SELECTOR SWITCHES.-The propeller selector switches located on the pilot's control pedestal (7 figure 15), provide for operation of the propellers in either automatic or fixed position. All flight operations should be made with the selector switches in the "AUTO CONSTANT SPEED" position. The selective fixed pitch positions of "DEC RPM" and "INC RPM" are used for various ground operations or if the constant speed control becomes inoperative. The "DEC RPM" and "INC RPM" positions are momentary.

    c. PROPELLER SYNCHRONIZER CONTROL.-The propeller synchronizer control lever at the left of the pilot's control pedestal (23 figure 15) controls the speed of both engines when the propeller selector switches are in the "AUTO" position. Moving the lever to the full "DEC RPM" position turns the master motor "OFF"

    d. MASTER SYNCHRONIZER MOTOR TACHOMETER.-A tachometer (19 figure 3) is located on the pilot's instrument panel for indicating RPM of engines when the selector switches are in "AUTO CONSTANT SPEED" position.

    e. PROPELLER FEATHER SWITCHES.-The propeller feather switches, one for each propeller (4 figure 15) are located on the pilot's control pedestal. The positions indicated are "FEATHER" and "NORMAL". The switches must be in "NORMAL" position except for feathering operations.

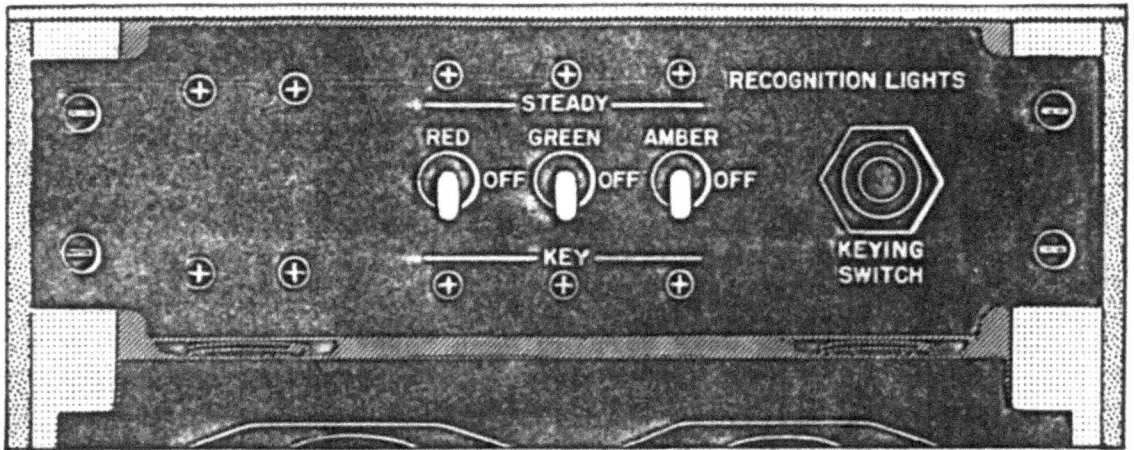

Figure 13 - Recognition Light Control Panel.

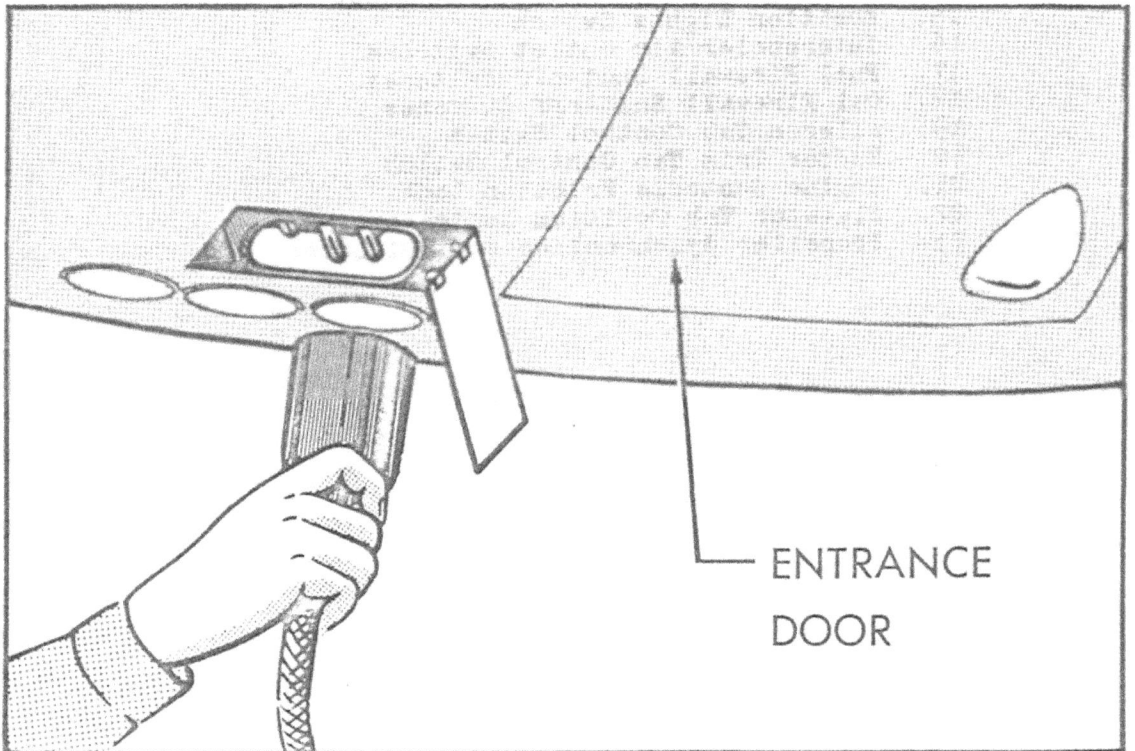

Figure 14 - External Power Supply Connection.

PILOT'S CONTROL PEDESTAL & SWITCH PANEL

Key to Figure 15.

1.   Oil Temperature Switches
2.   Cowl Flap Switches
3.   Turbo Boost Selector Switches
4.   Propeller Feathering Switches
5.   Landing Gear Warning Horn "OFF" Switch
6.   Propeller Synchronizer "OFF" Indicator Light
7.   Propeller Selector Switches
8.   Throttles
9.   Microphone Switch Button
10. Mixture Controls
11. Elevator Trim Tab Control
12. Wing Flap Control Handle
13. Landing Lights Switches
14. Landing Light Retraction Switches
15. Position Lights Switch
16. Intercooler Air Outlet Switches
17. Fuel Firewall Shut-off Switches
18. Oil Firewall Shut-off Switches
19. Aileron Tab Control Switch
20. Rudder Trim Tab Control Switch
21. Engine Controls Friction Lock
22. Elevator Tab Position Indicator
23. Propeller Synchronizer Control Lever

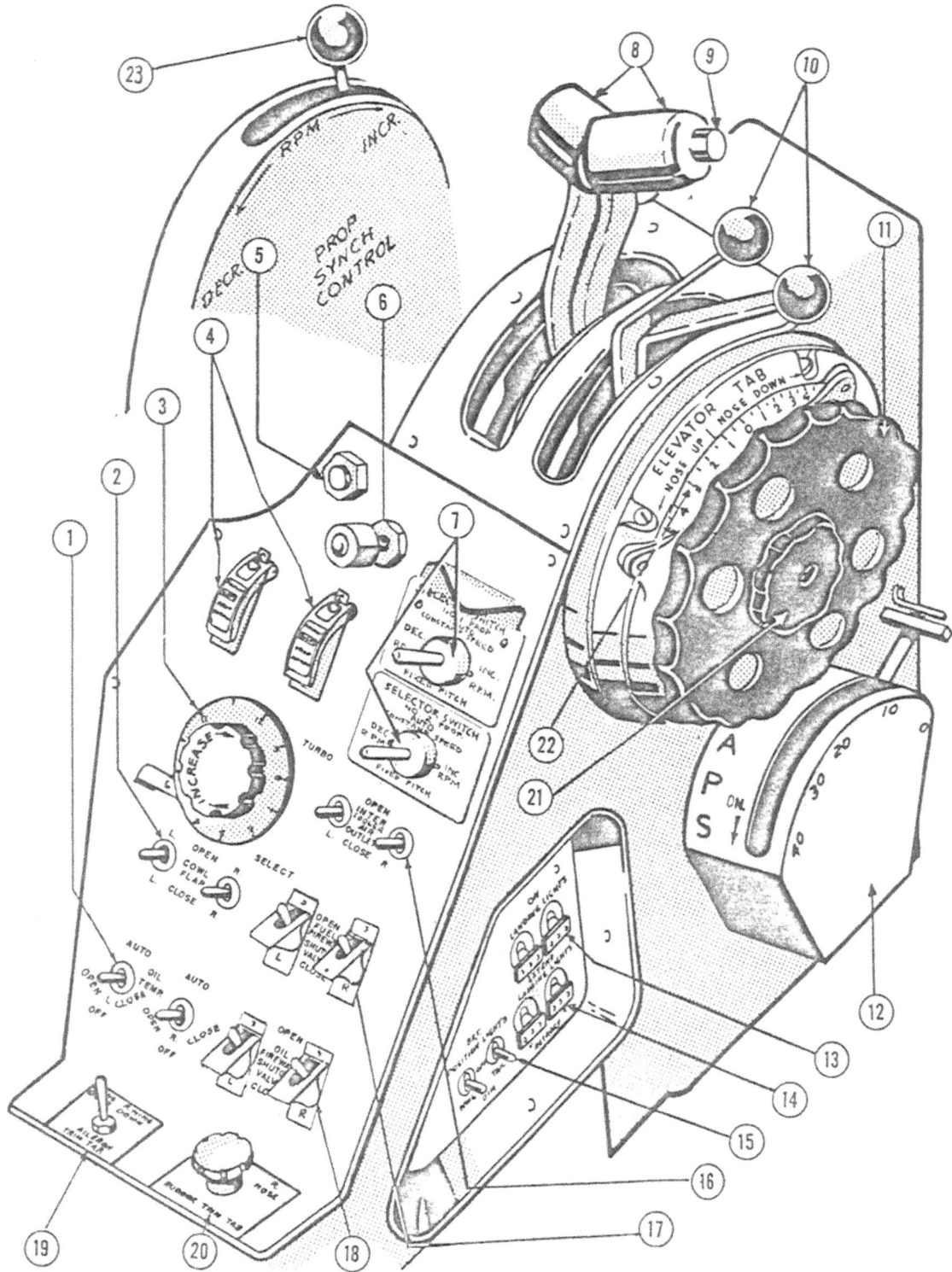

Figure 15 - Pilot's Control Pedestal & Switch Panel.

NOTE

The pilot can also feather by holding the selector
switch in the "DEC RPM" position until the blades
reach the feather angle. This can only be done
with the feather switch in the "NORMAL" position
and will give normal pitch change rate instead of
fast rate.

f. PROPELLER CONTROL CIRCUIT BREAKERS.-The four propeller
control circuit breakers consisting of one "VOLTAGE BOOSTER CIRCUIT
BREAKER", two "SELECTOR SWITCH CIRCUIT BREAKERS", and one
"SYNCHRONIZER CIRCUIT BREAKER" all located on the pilot's instrument panel. (See 37 figure 7.)

1-12. COWL FLAPS.-The electrically operated cowl flaps are controlled by two switches (2 figure 15) located on the pedestal
switch panel. The switches are spring loaded in the "OPEN" and
"CLOSE" positions.

1-13. MISCELLANEOUS EQUIPMENT.

a. RELIEF TUBE.-The pilot's relief tube (18 figure 6) is
located on the right side of the control column base. The relief
tube shut-off valve (23 figure 6) is located under the right side
of the pilot's seat. This valve must be closed when not in use
while the cabin is pressurized.

b. DISPOSAL RELIEF CONTAINERS.-Two disposal relief containers
are located on the right-hand side of the fuselage.

c. SHOULDER HARNESS AND SAFETY BELTS.-A shoulder harness and
safety belt are provided for the pilot's and navigator's seats.
A safety belt only is provided for the photographer's seat.

d. THERMOS BOTTLES.-Two thermos bottles (18 figure 4) are
stowed on the right side of the fuselage.

e. ANTI-GLARE CURTAINS.-A curtain is provided to prevent light
from the pilot's compartment entering the navigator's compartment
during night flights, and is stowed on the right side of the tunnel
beneath the pilot's seat. (See 18 figure 21.)

f. SUN VISORS.-Two sun visors are provided for the crew, and
are stowed, one to the left of the pilot's seat and one on the
right side of the tunnel beneath the pilot's seat. (See 18 and 19
figure 21.)

g. COVERS.-Covers are provided for engine, propellers, wings,
nose, and canopy, and are stowed in the baggage compartment located
in the right boom aft of the landing gear well.

h. "G" FILE STOWAGE.-Two aircraft data cases are located in the baggage compartment in the right boom.

i. MAP AND DATA CASE.-The map and data case are installed in the cockpit, back of the pilot's seat, underneath the navigator's table. (See 11 figure 10.)

j. PYROTECHNIC PISTOL.-The pyrotechnic pistol mount with pistol holder and cartridge case is located to the right of the navigator's seat. (See 15 and 16 figure 4.)

k. BAGGAGE COMPARTMENT.-The baggage compartment is located in the right boom back of the landing gear well. Entrance is gained through the landing gear well.

S E C T I O N   II.

N O R M A L   O P E R A T I N G   I N S T R U C T I O N S

NOTE

Sufficient space has been provided after
each paragraph in this section for
pilot's notes on aircraft performance
or operation.

2-1. BEFORE ENTERING PILOT'S COMPARTMENT.

   a. RESTRICTIONS.

   (1) FLIGHT RESTRICTIONS.-The following maneuvers are
strictly prohibited:

      Loop   Inverted flight
      Spin   Vertical dive
      Roll   Vertical bank
              Immelmann

   Maximum allowable engine RPM 3060 for 30 seconds.

   (2) TAKE-OFF WEIGHT LIMITATIONS.

   Maximum recommended take-off weight - 60,000.

   Maximum capacity of the baggage compartment is 250
pounds.

   (3) AIRSPEED LIMITATIONS.

      (a) Maximum allowable indicated airspeed - do not exceed:

      390 I.A.S.   0 - 5,000 feet.
      360 I.A.S.   5,000 - 25,000 feet.
      290 I.A.S.   25,000 - 35,000 feet.

      (b) Restrictions for lowering flaps - do not exceed:

      200 I.A.S. with flaps extended - 20°.
      170 I.A.S. with flaps full-down- 40°.

(<u>c</u>) Restrictions for lowering landing gear:

Do not start to lower gear above 170 I.A.S.
Do not exceed 170 I.A.S. with gear down.

(4) GROUND OPERATING LIMITATIONS.

Do not operate above 1000 RPM until oil temperature has exceeded 40°C.

Do not exceed cylinder head temperature of 232°C.

<u>b</u>. Check Form 1.

<u>c</u>. Check Form F., weight and balance clearance, AN 01-1-40.

<u>d</u>. ADDITIONAL CHECKS.

(1) Before entering the pilot's compartment, check to see that the airplane has been serviced with fuel, oil, hydraulic fluid, oxygen, and photographic film.

(2) All covers - removed.

(3) Wheel chocks - in place.

(4) External power connected if available.

<u>e</u>. HOW TO GAIN ENTRANCE.-The entrance door is located on the lower right side of the fuselage. Depress and turn the handle to open the door. A handrail is provided at the aft end of the hatch. Upon reaching the step on the door, pull the ladder up with your foot. After gaining entrance, pull the door up with the lanyard and lock it by pulling the inside handle outboard against the stop. (See figure 19.)

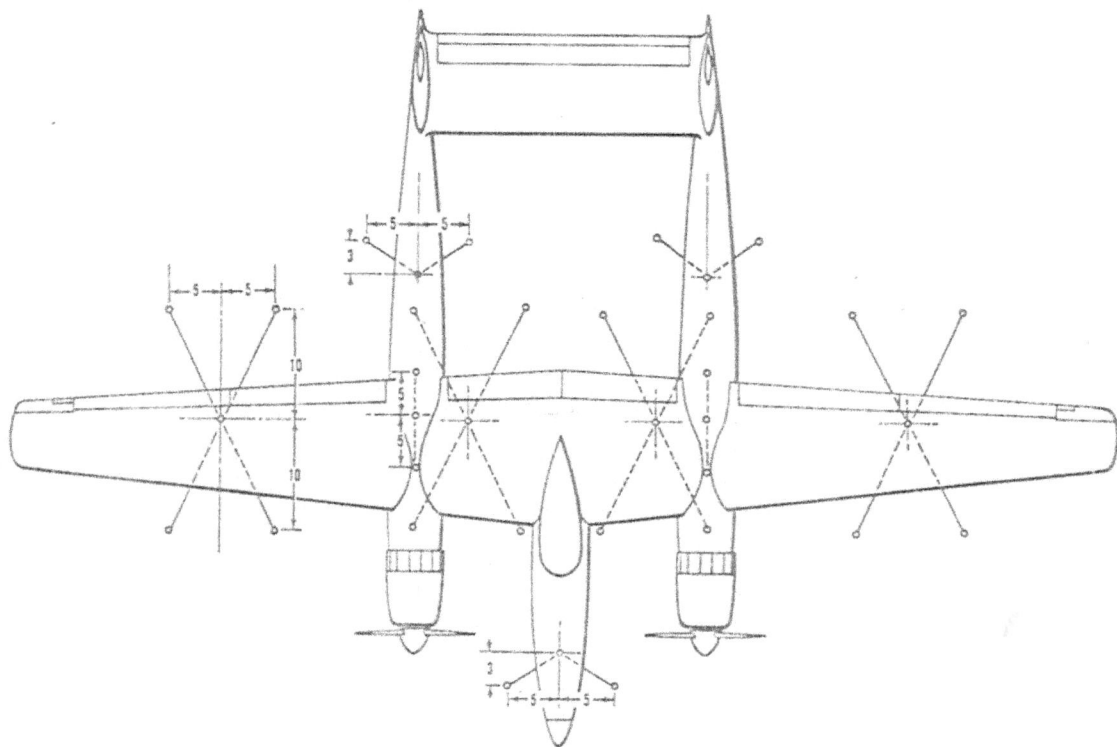

Figure 16 - Mooring Diagram.

2-2.   ON ENTERING PILOT'S COMPARTMENT.

   <u>a</u>.   STANDARD CHECK.

     (1)   Disengage surface controls lock and stow.

     (2)   All switches - "OFF".

     (3)   Generator - "OFF".

     (4)   Adjust rudder pedals and seat position.

     (5)   Loose equipment - secured.

     (6)   Thermos bottles - filled.

     (7)   Clock - set.

     (8)   Altimeter - set.

     (9)   Check canopy locks.

     (10)   Master Battery and Ignition Switch "BATT. ON - IGN ON".

     (11)   Inverter switches "ON".

     (12)   Radio equipment - check.

     (13)   Landing gear lights - GREEN - "LOCKED DOWN".

     (14)   Landing gear - "NEUTRAL".

     (15)   Parking brakes - "LOCKED".

     (16)   Fuel Selector switches - check fuel pressures on
each selector separately with the other "OFF" and engines
stopped.

        "ON" - no pressure.

        "LOW" - 12 psi.

        "HI" - 25 psi.

     (17)   Cabin air controls vent - "OPEN".   Turbos -
"CLOSED".

     (18)   Check fuel.

(19) Check instruments.

(20) Pitot heater - as required.

(21) For night flights - check all lights.

2-3. FUEL SYSTEM MANAGEMENT.

   <u>a</u>. NORMAL OPERATION.-Fuel is normally supplied to the left and
right engines from the corresponding left and right tank groups,
including drop tanks. When necessary cross-feed lines permit
fuel transfer from one group of tanks to an opposite engine. Fuel
control is through fuel tank selector switches, a cross-feed switch,
and drop tank fuel transfer valve switches.

   <u>b</u>. FUEL TANK SELECTOR SWITCHES.-The fuel tank selector switches
"LEFT OUTBOARD", "LEFT INBOARD", "RIGHT INBOARD", and "RIGHT
OUTBOARD", indicate the four groups of wing fuel tanks from which
fuel is to be drawn. (See figures 17 and 18.) All tanks in each
selected group are drained simultaneously. For take-off move
desired tank group selector switch (figures 8, and 17) to "ON",
to open the tank selector valve, and then to "LO BOOST" to obtain
the required fuel pressure. Move selector switch to "HI BOOST"
for cross-feed operation or when flying at high altitude.

   <u>c</u>. CROSS-FEED.-Although fuel cannot be transferred from one
group of tanks to the other, fuel can be supplied to either or
both engines from any group of tanks. Fuel is one group of tanks
is supplied to the engine on the opposite side of the airplane by
moving the cross-feed switch (figures 8 and 18) to "OPEN" and the
selected tank group selector switch to "HI BOOST".

   <u>d</u>. FUEL DROP TANKS.-Fuel from the drop tanks is transferred
to the corresponding outboard tanks by moving the left or right
fuel transfer switches to "ON". The transfer switch may be left
on until the "DROP TANK EMPTY" light comes on. To release drop
tanks after emptying, move guarded release switches on pilot's
left switch panel to "ON". (See figure 8.)

   <u>e</u>. FUEL TANK SEQUENCE. Fuel tanks will be used in the following
order: (See figure 17.)

     (1) Drop tanks.

     (2) Inboard tanks.

     (3) Outboard tanks.

RESTRICTED

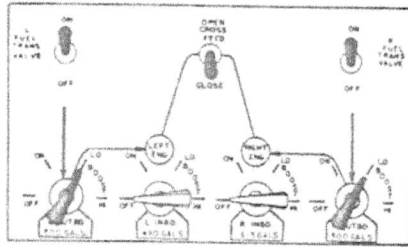

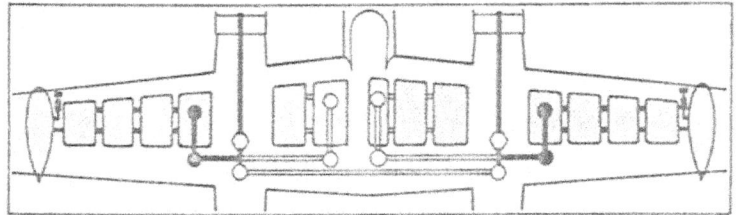

1. RIGHT AND LEFT DROPPABLE TANKS Both Fuel Transfer Switches ON and Outboard Sump Pumps LOW

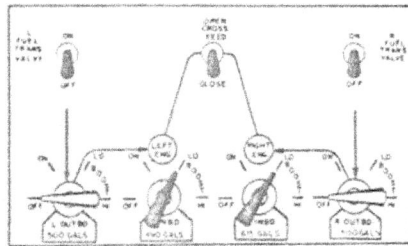

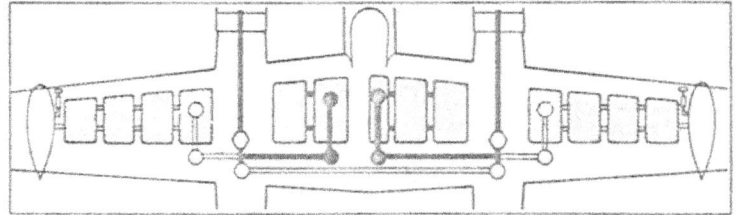

2. RIGHT AND LEFT INBOARD TANKS Inboard Sump Pump Switches LOW, All Other Switches OFF

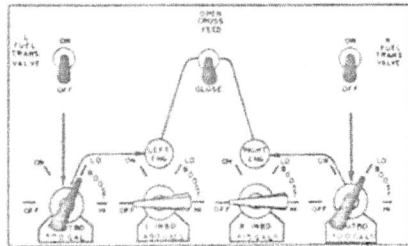

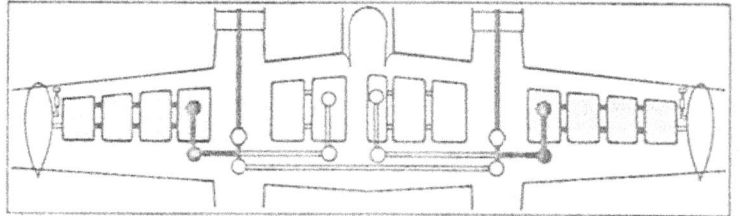

3. RIGHT AND LEFT OUTBOARD TANKS Fuel Transfer Switches OFF. Both Outboard Sump Pump Switches LOW

Figure 17 - Fuel Tank Sequence Diagram.

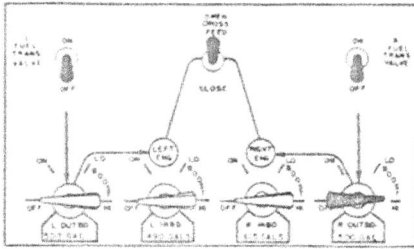

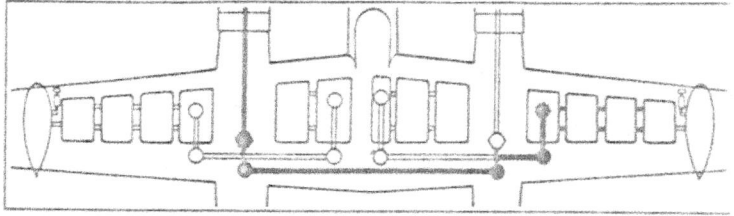

1. LEFT ENGINE OPERATION ON RIGHT OUTBOARD FUEL TANKS

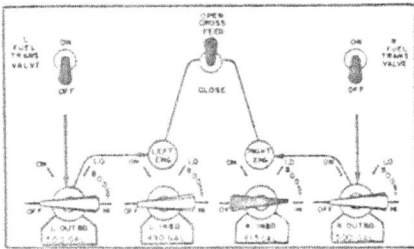

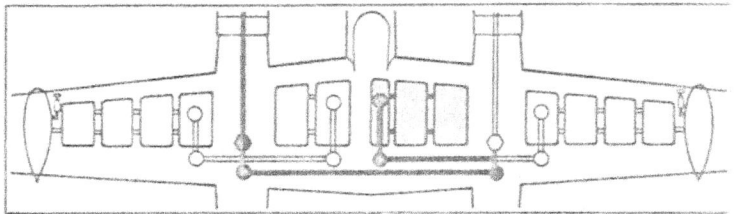

2. LEFT ENGINE OPERATION ON RIGHT INBOARD FUEL TANKS

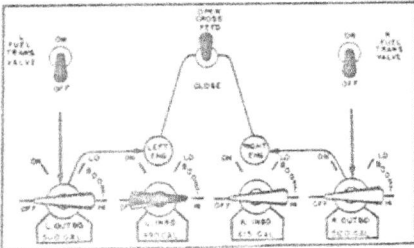

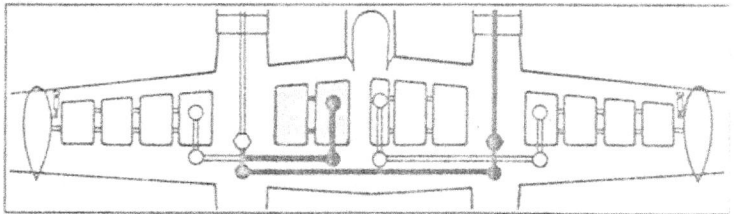

3. RIGHT ENGINE OPERATION ON LEFT INBOARD FUEL TANKS

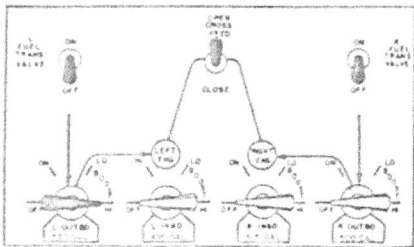

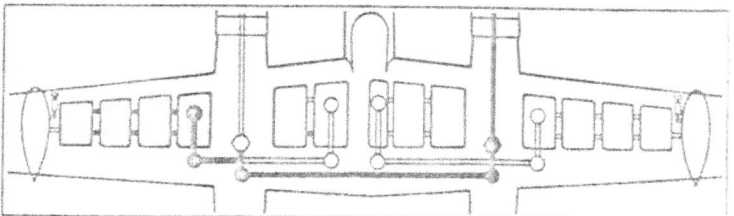

4. RIGHT ENGINE OPERATION ON LEFT OUTBOARD FUEL TANKS

Figure 18 - Fuel Cross Feed Diagram.

2-4.   STARTING ENGINE.

WARNING

All engine starts must be made by priming
only, and the mixture control must be kept
in "IDLE CUT-OFF" until the engine is
firing on the prime. If the mixture control
is moved out of "IDLE CUT-OFF" too soon,
fuel will collect in the long, upward
sloping intake pipes. This fuel will
remain idle in the intake pipes until a
critical engine speed is reached at which
point all the collected fuel will be drawn
at once into the engine. The amount can
be sufficient to "Hydraulic" the engine.
Under no circumstances should the mixture
control be moved from "IDLE CUT-OFF" until
the engine is firing on the prime.

CAUTION

If loading of the lower cylinders is
suspected, remove the lower spark plugs
before turning propellers over.

a.   STARTING PROCEDURE.

(1) Master Battery and Ingition Switch - "OFF".

(2) Individual Ignition Switches - "OFF".

(3) Generator Switches - "OFF".

(4) Mixture controls - "IDLE CUT-OFF".

(5) Propeller feather switches - "NORMAL".

(6) Have propeller pulled through 10 blades.

(7) Propeller circuit breaker switches (4) all - "ON".
(See 37 figure 7.)

(8) Propeller selector switches - "AUTO".

(9) Propeller synchronizer control lever - "FULL INCR".

(10) Oil temperature - "AUTOMATIC".

Figure 19 - Airplane Entrance Door & Ladder.

(11) Cowl flaps - full "OPEN".

(12) Intercooler air outlet switches - "CLOSE".

(13) Carburetor air filters - "AUTOMATIC".

(14) Oil firewall shut-off switches (2) - "OPEN".

(15) Fuel firewall shut-off switches (2) - "OPEN".

(16) Carburetor air heat - "FULL DECREASE".

(17) Exhaust shut-off - "OPEN".

(18) Turbo boost - set at "0".

(19) Fuel cross feed - "CLOSE".

(20) R. and L. fuel transfer - "OFF".

(21) Fuel tank selectors, left and right - "LO BOOST".

(22) Throttle - cracked.

(23) Master Batt & Ign switch - "IGN ON BATT ON".

(24) Inverters - "ON".

(25) Ignition switches - "BOTH".

(26) Primer switch - as required.

(27) Start on prime - right engine first.

(28) Mixture control - move with moderate motion to "AUTO RICH" after engine starts.

(29) Throttle - 1000 RPM.

(30) Oil pressure - watch for rise; if none indicated within 30 seconds STOP engine.

(31) Disconnect external power.

(32) Generator switches - "ON".

b. WARM ENGINE.-Overloading of a warm engine may be indicated by a discharge of fuel from the engine drain lines. Do not attempt to restart until fuel has ceased to drain. The most frequent cause of overloading is failure to return mixture control into "IDLE CUT-OFF" after a false start.

c. COLD ENGINE.-With a cold engine, overloading is indicated essentially by the presence of liquid gasoline in the exhaust. Allow all liquid fuel to clear drain lines, then crank engine with open throttle for a dozen revolutions with the ignition off.

NOTE

If fuel vapor odor is not present in exhaust, engine may not have been given sufficient prime. Use additional priming cautiously and repeat starting procedure. If it is still not possible to start, shut down and investigate.

2-5. WARM-UP AND GROUND TESTS.

a. WARM-UP.-After first half minute, warm-up with propeller control lever in "INCREASE RPM" and engine speed of 1000 RPM. Long continued idling below 800 RPM may result in fouled spark plugs. Short periods of idling at 400 or 500 RPM may be used with occasional run-up for cleaning out.

b. GROUND TESTS.

(1) GENERAL.-When oil temperature is above 40°C., open throttle to 30 in. Hg or about 2000 RPM, with the propeller control lever in "INCREASE RPM".

CAUTION

Do not operate above 1000 RPM until the
oil-in temperature has exceeded 40°C.

(2) MAGNETO CHECK.-With propeller selector switch in "FIXED PITCH" open throttle to 2000 RPM, 30 in. Hg and test each magneto. Normal drop 60-80 RPM. Maximum drop 100 RPM.

(3) TEMPERATURE AND PRESSURE INDICATORS.

(a) Do not exceed 204°C. Cylinder head temperature during normal ground operation.

(b) Hydraulic pressure - 1250-1500 psi.

(4) MANIFOLD PRESSURE DRAIN (36 figure 7) - "PUSH" L. and R.

(5) FUEL SYSTEM.-Check operation of each tank group and cross-feed. Fuel pressure - 24-27 psi. Resume normal operating procedure.

(6) OIL TEMPERATURE SWITCHES.-With assistance of an observer, check operation of doors in "OPEN", "CLOSED", and "AUTO" positions of switches.

(7) WING FLAPS.-Lower flaps to 40°, then retract.

(8) RADIO (1 PHASE) INVERTER SWITCH.-Test main inverter by throwing switch to main inverter. The "BOTH INV. OUT" indicator light on instrument panel light shield (9 figure 3) should go out. Test spare inverter by throwing switch to "SPARE TEST" (figure 8). The "BOTH INV. OUT" indicator on instrument panel light shield should again go out. Return switch to main inverter.

(9) GYRO INSTRUMENTS - uncaged.

(10) AUTO PILOT (3 PHASE) INVERTER SWITCH.-Turn switch to "INV. #1". In about 30 seconds a slight change in heading may be noted on the Master Compass Indicator. Turn switch off and in about 2 or 3 minutes repeat with switch in "INV. #2" position. Return switch to "INV. #1" position.

(11) BOOM CAMERA HEAT SWITCH.-"ON" and check.

(12) TURBOSUPERCHARGERS.-Open throttle to 30 in Hg. and set turbo boost selector at "8". Turbos will not operate below 30 in Hg.

(13) INTERCOOLER.-Check operation of flap.

(14) COWL FLAPS.- Check for operation.

(15) TRIM TABS.-Check for operation.

(16) ENTRANCE HATCH.-Closed and latched.

2-6. TAXIING.

a. GENERAL.-Observe normal tricycle landing gear taxiing procedure.

2-7. BEFORE TAKE-OFF.

a. Propeller RPM - full "INCREASE".

b. Turbo boost selector (3 figure 15) - set at "8", (with "Filtered Air", set at "0").

c. Operate circuit breaker reset (30 figure 7).

d. Trim tabs - as required for take-off.

e. Hydraulic pressure - 1250-1500 psi.

f. Fuel tank selectors (figure 8), fullest tank, left and right, "LO BOOST".

g. Adjust engine controls friction lock.

h. Mixture controls - "AUTO RICH".

i. Propeller check - Propeller synchronizer control to full "INCREASE", throttle to 2000 RPM - propeller synchronizer control back to 1700 RPM on synchronizer tachometer. Note engine tachometer back to 1700; propeller synchronizer control to full "INCREASE" rapidly. Note no increase in engine RPM until synchronizer tachometer reaches take off RPM. Decrease and increase RPM manually and note if engine RPM responds. Momentarily operate Feather Switch and note engine RPM decrease. Return propeller selector switch to "AUTO CONSTANT SPEED".

j. Carburetor air temperature - max. 40°C.

k. Oil pressure - normal 80-85 psi 2000 RPM.

l. Oil temperature - Min. 40°C. Max. 85°C.

m. Fuel Pressure - 25-27 psi 2000 RPM.

n. Check engines at take-off RPM and manifold pressure - set propellers for 2700 RPM.

o. Flaps - set 20° for take-off.

p. Release brakes.

2-8. TAKE-OFF. (Refer to figure 30 for operating data.)

   a. Throttles - 53.5 in. Hg.

   b. Engine RPM - 2700 RPM (five minutes maximum).

   c. Landing gear - "UP". Return to "NEUTRAL" after landing gear Red Light is out.

   d. Wing flaps - "UP".

   e. Cowl flaps - as required for proper cylinder temperature.

   f. Oil temperature switch - "AUTOMATIC" or as required.

   g. Fuel tank sequence - drop tanks, inboard tanks, outboard tanks.

   h. Reduce manifold pressure to 45.5 in. Hg. at 2550 RPM after clearing all obstacles.

   i. Observe instrument and operational limitations.

2-9. ENGINE FAILURE DURING TAKE-OFF.

   a. ON THE GROUND.

     (1) Throttle - "CLOSE".

     (2) Apply brakes.

     (3) Master battery and ignition switch - "OFF".

     (4) If running off runway - release drop tanks and retract landing gear.

     (5) Jettison rear canopy to escape if wheels are retracted.

<u>b</u>.   IN THE AIR.

   (1) ONE ENGINE.

      (<u>a</u>) Hard rudder opposite dead engine.

      (<u>b</u>) Landing gear - "UP".

      (<u>c</u>) Propellers - "FEATHER" (dead engine).

      (<u>d</u>) Flaps - "UP".

      (<u>e</u>) Drop tanks - "RELEASE".

      (<u>f</u>) Cowl flaps - "CLOSE" (dead engine).

      (<u>g</u>) Turn fuel tank and ignition - "OFF" (dead engine).

      (<u>h</u>) Mixture control - "IDLE CUT-OFF" (dead engine).

   (2) BOTH ENGINES.

      (<u>a</u>) Landing gear - "UP".

      (<u>b</u>) Drop tanks - "RELEASE".

      (<u>c</u>) Wing flaps - 40°.

      (<u>d</u>) Master battery and ignition switch - "OFF".

      (<u>e</u>) Mixture controls - "IDLE CUT-OFF".

      (<u>f</u>) If possible jettison rear canopy.

      (<u>g</u>) Lock shoulder harness.

      (<u>h</u>) Land straight ahead.

2-10. CLIMB - NORMAL RATED POWER. (Refer to figure 32 for climb data.)

a. PROCEDURE.

(1) Cowl flap switches - "OPEN" (as required).

(2) Engine speed at 2550 RPM.

(3) Manifold pressure - 45.5 in. Hg.

(4) Cylinder head temperature - 232°C. Max.

(5) Oil temperature - 60°-95°C.

(6) Oil pressure - 80-85 psi.

(7) Turbo - as required.

(8) Carburetor air - 38°C. "OPEN" or "CLOSE" intercooler air flap as required.

2-11. DURING FLIGHT.

a. GENERAL.-Refer to figures 33 and 34 for flight operation data.

b. CARBURETOR HEAT.-At altitude where turbos are being used, carburetor air temperature may be regulated by adjusting intercooler air outlet flap.

WARNING

To apply carburetor heat when the cabin
is being pressurized, first discontinue
cabin pressurizing; second, move "CARB.
HEAT" switch to "INCREASE" as required.
When necessity for carburetor heat is
past, move "CARB. HEAT" switch to
"DECREASE" until hot air valve is closed,
return to "OFF" and continue cabin pressurizing.

RESTRICTED

2-12. STALLS.

POWER OFF STALLING SPEEDS
AT VARIOUS GROSS WEIGHTS

GROSS WEIGHT	FLAP SETTINGS		
	0°	20°	40°
39,600	105	95	85
47,500	116	104	93
60,000	130	117	104

2-13. SPINS. (to be issued when available.)

2-14. PERMISSIBLE ACROBATICS. (None.)

2-15. DIVING. (to be issued when available.)

2-16. APPROACH AND LANDING. (Refer to "TAKE-OFF, CLIMB, and LANDING CHART", figure 32.)

a. During the initial approach, perform the following operations:

(1) Fuel tank selector, fullest tank, "LO BOOST".

(2) Mixture control - "AUTO RICH".

(3) Prop Synchronizer Controls - "FULL INCREASE".

(4) Exhaust shutoff - "OPEN".

(5) Turbo boost - set at "0".

(6) Hydraulic pressure - 1250-1500.

(7) Cowl flaps - "CLOSED".

(8) Carb. air filters - "AUTOMATIC".

(9) Landing gear - "DOWN", landing gear lights - "GREEN". (Do not lower above 170 MPH.)

(10) Wing flaps - 40°. (Do not lower above 170 MPH.)

(11) Before taxiing - Cowl flaps "OPEN", wing flaps "UP".

2-17. STOPPING ENGINE.

   a. PROCEDURE.

     (1) Cylinder temperature - 177°C. Maximum for shutdown.

     (2) Oil dilution - as required.

     (3) Mixture control - "IDLE CUT-OFF" at 1000 RPM.

     (4) Throttle - "OPEN" - Master Batt. & Ign. - "OFF".

     (5) Landing gear - "NEUTRAL".

2-18. BEFORE LEAVING PILOT'S COMPARTMENT.

   a. Cowl flaps - "CLOSE" in cold weather after engines have cooled. "OPEN" in warm weather.

   b. Parking brakes - set (after cooled).

    <u>c</u>. All switches - "OFF".

    <u>d</u>. Surface control lock - engaged.

    <u>e</u>. Entrance hatch - closed.

PILOT'S NOTES

S E C T I O N   III

E M E R G E N C Y   O P E R A T I N G   I N S T R U C T I O N S

3-1. EMERGENCY ESCAPE.

a. EMERGENCY EXITS.-The two emergency exits are the detachable aft section of the canopy (2 figure 21) and the main entrance hatch.

WARNING

The fuselage must be depressurized before
a safe exit can be made.

(1) CANOPY - AFT SECTION.

(a) Break safety wire on release lever (2 figure 21).

(b) Pull release lever "UP".

(c) Push window aft, then push canopy aft and free.

NOTE

A flush skin handle, located left of top
center on the outside at the aft canopy
retaining strip, is provided for
emergency release of the canopy for
entrance on the ground.

(2) ENTRANCE HATCH - EMERGENCY OPERATION.

(a) Entrance hatch jettison lever (25 figure 6) - rotate clockwise and pull.

(b) Bail out facing aft.

3-2. FIRE.

a. ENGINE FIRES IN FLIGHT.-Make sure following controls are used for engine afire only:

(1) Cowl flaps - "OPEN".

5

(2) Firewall fuel shut-off valve - "CLOSE".

(3) Firewall oil shut-off valve - "CLOSE".

(4) Propeller - "FEATHER".

(5) Ignition - "OFF".

(6) CO_2 fire extinguisher - "ON".

(7) Do not start engine again.

(8) Land as soon as possible.

(9) Cowl flaps - "CLOSE" after fire is out.

(10) Cabin air controls - "CLOSE" left or right turbo depending on which side fire is located.

b. FUSELAGE FIRES.-Use portable CO_2 fire extinguisher (1 figure 4). Operating instructions are on the cylinder.

3-3. ENGINE FAILURE DURING FLIGHT.

a. ONE ENGINE.-Accomplish the following instructions for the dead engine only.

(1) Propeller - "FEATHER".

(2) Throttle - "CLOSE".

(3) Mixture control - "IDLE CUT-OFF".

(4) Fuel selector - "OFF".

(5) Cowl flaps - "CLOSED".

(6) Ignition - "OFF".

(7) Retrim airplane.

(8) Do not turn firewall shut-off valves to "CLOSE" if engine can be restarted safely.

NOTE

If, in flight, it becomes necessary to turn off the complete electrical system and still leave the engines running, turn the master switch full clockwise to the "IGN ON" position marked in red.

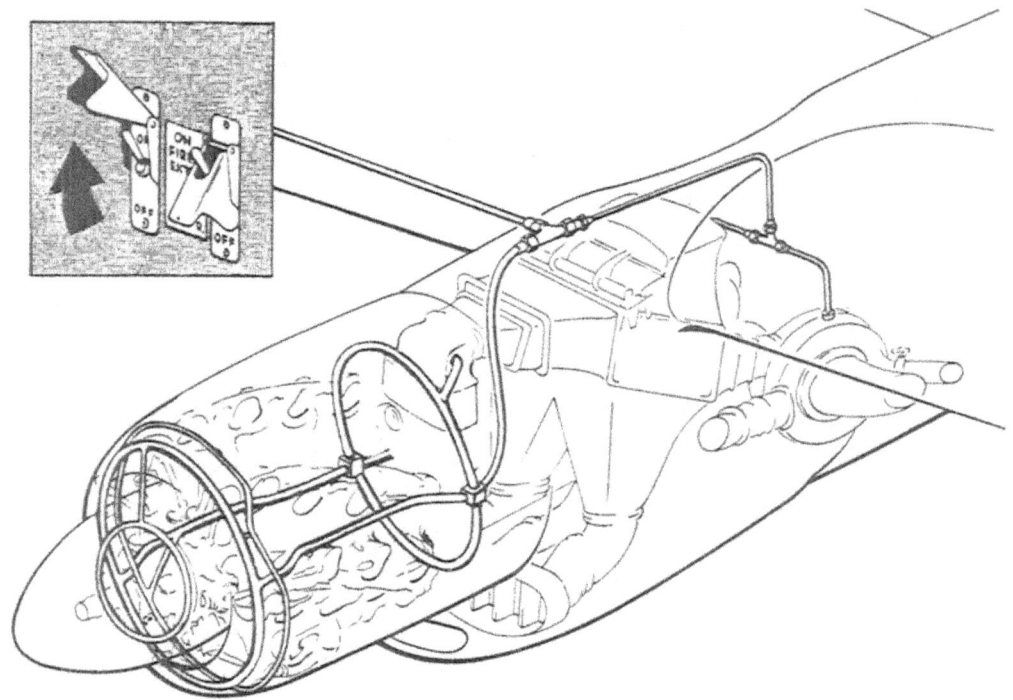

Figure 20 - Engine Fire Extinguisher.

b. LANDING WITH ONE (OR BOTH) ENGINES INOPERATIVE.

(1) With both engines dead, the airplane should be abandoned if the altitude permits; otherwise, it should be brought in for a belly landing. (Refer to paragraph 6 this section.)

(2) For single engine landing, shut down dead engine completely and proceed with normal landing.

3-4. LANDING GEAR EMERGENCY OPERATION.-In an emergency, lower the landing gear by moving the landing gear control lever to "DOWN" and the electrical hydraulic system switch to "ON" (figure 8).

3-5. BRAKE EMERGENCY OPERATION.

a. Emergency hydraulic switch (figure 8) - "ON".

b. Emergency brake lever (20 figure 6) - Pull up.

c. Rotate brake lever left or right for differential brake control.

3-6. LANDING WITH WHEELS RETRACTED.

a. Drop tanks - "RELEASE" if installed.

b. Wing flaps - 20° below 200 I.A.S.

CAUTION

Do not lower flaps more than 20° above 170 I.A.S.

c. Wing flaps - 40° when landing is assured.

d. Gradually reduce power and trim for landing.

3-7. LANDING IN WATER (DITCHING).-When altitude permits, the airplane should be abandoned rather than ditched.

a. BAILING OUT OVER WATER.

(1) PILOT'S DUTIES.-When the pilot has made the decision to bail out over water, the following preparations for abandoning the airplane must be made.

(a) Command navigator to send SOS message.

(b) Release drop tanks, if installed. Empty tanks may be life saver if rafts are lost.

RESTRICTED

(c) Attach one C-2 life raft (1 figure 6) to parachute harness and bail out through fuselage exit.

(2) NAVIGATOR'S DUTIES.-When the signal for bailing out is received, navigator must perform the following ditching procedures:

(a) At command of pilot, send SOS message.

(b) Attach one C-2 life raft (1 figure 6) to parachute harness.

(c) Jettison aft canopy and entrance hatch.

(d) Attach static line of dinghy radio to airplane, then throw the dinghy radio overboard.

(e) At command of pilot, bail out through entrance hatch.

b. PREPARATION FOR DITCHING.

(1) PILOT'S DUTIES.

(a) Ditch airplane before fuel is exhausted in order to maintain power during ditching operation.

(b) Lower flaps 20°.

(c) Check landing gear "UP".

(d) Command crew member to jettison aft canopy.

(e) Release drop tanks, if installed.

(f) Command crew member to ascertain that entrance hatch is locked.

(g) Use engines to flatten out approach.

(h) With only one engine available, use only a little power to flatten approach.

CAUTION

Do not open up engine during final
stages of ditching.

RESTRICTED

(1) Be sure the shoulder harness and safety belt are fastened securely as there is a violent deceleration of the airplane upon final impact.

(i) Land into the wind. As soon as the airplane comes to rest, get out immediately through the canopy exit as the airplane will probably sink rapidly.

(2) NAVIGATOR'S DUTIES.

(a) Send SOS message.

(b) At command of pilot, jettison aft canopy, and check that entrance hatch is locked.

(c) Take ditching station in navigator's seat.

(d) Fasten safety belt and shoulder harness.

(e) As soon as airplane comes to rest, break out life rafts and dinghy radio after clearing canopy. Leave airplane through canopy exit immediately.

c. DITCHING CHARACTERISTICS. (To be issued when available.)

3-8. MISCELLANEOUS EMERGENCY EQUIPMENT.

a. PYROTECHNIC PISTOL.-The pistol with mount, 12 signal flares, and signal flare containers are installed to the right and above the entrance hatch. The pistol must be fired while in the mount. (See figure 21.)

b. LOCATION OF AXE.-A hand axe is stowed on the right side of the pilot's compartment. (See 19 figure 4.)

c. EMERGENCY PRESSURE WARNING HORN.-An automatic emergency pressure warning horn (22 figure 4), sounds an intermittent tone when the cabin pressure drops below the standard altitude pressure of 12,000 feet. The warning horn shut-off button (figure 23) is mounted on the cabin air control panel.

d. EMERGENCY CABIN PRESSURE DUMP VALVE.-The cabin pressure dump valve lever (figure 23) is located on the cabin air control panel. Cabin pressure may be dropped to normal flight pressure in five to twenty seconds with the full airflow from each turbo entering the cabin.

EMERGENCY EQUIPMENT AND EXITS DIAGRAM

Key to Figure 21.

1.   Dinghy Radio
2.   Aft Canopy Release
3.   Life Rafts (2)
4.   Spare Inverter Switch
4A. APS-13 Alarm Bell
5.   Emergency Hydraulic Pump Switch
6.   Engine Fire Extinguisher Controls
7.   Firewall Oil Shut-off Valve Switch
8.   Firewall Fuel Shut-off Valve Switch
9.   Propeller Feathering Switches
10. Propeller Selector Switches
11. Oxygen Regulator Emergency Control
12. APS-13 Warning Light
13. First Aid Kits (2)
14. Portable CO_2 Fire Extinguisher

14A. Hand Axe
15. Emergency Hydraulic Brake Control
16. Radio Demolition Switch
17. APS-13 Control
18. Sun Visor and Anti-Glare Curtain Container
19. Sun Visor Container
20. Entrance Hatch Jettison Lever
21. Oxygen Walk-Around Unit

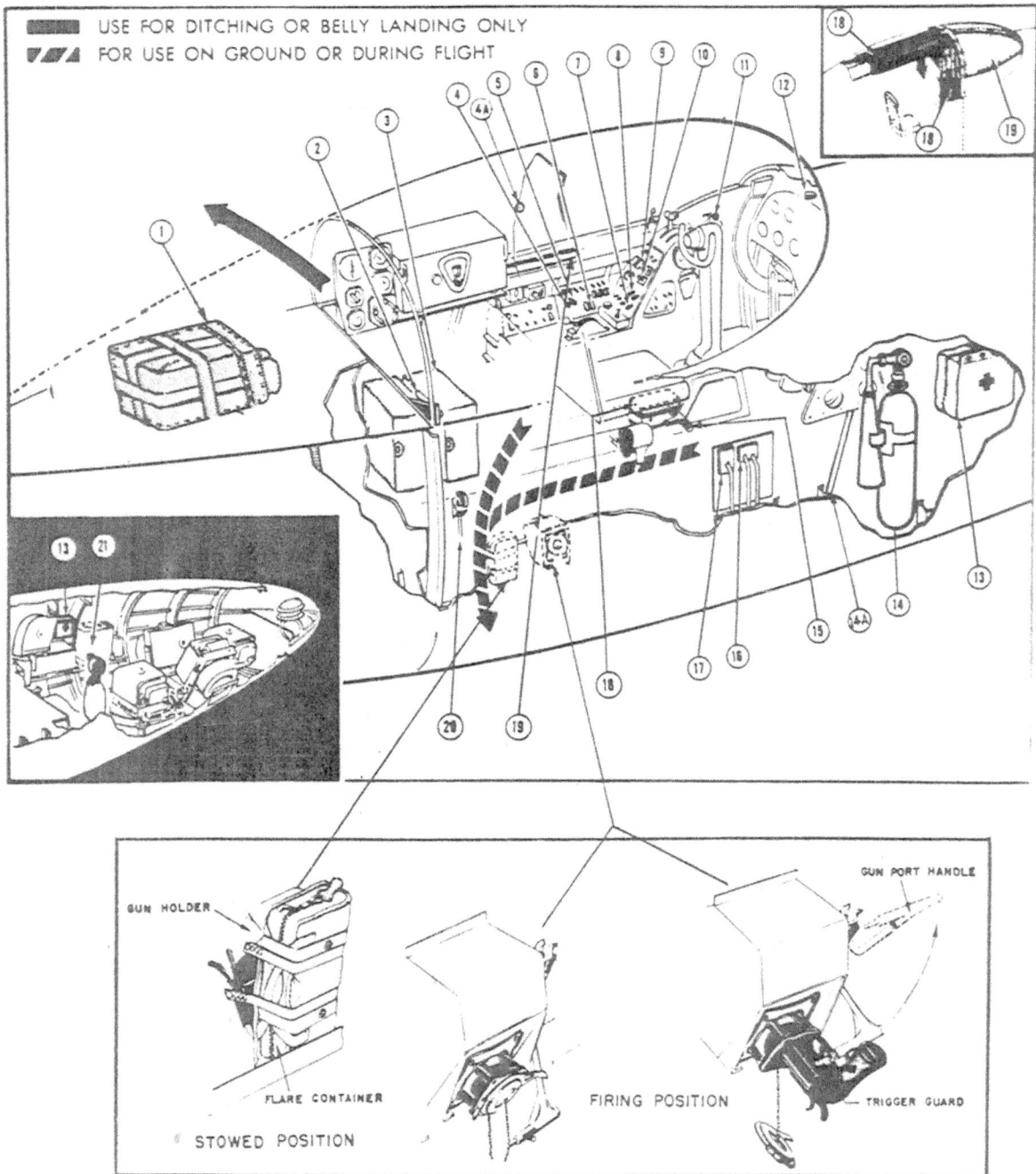

USE FOR DITCHING OR BELLY LANDING ONLY
FOR USE ON GROUND OR DURING FLIGHT

GUN HOLDER

FLARE CONTAINER

STOWED POSITION

FIRING POSITION

GUN PORT HANDLE

TRIGGER GUARD

Figure 21 - Emergency Equipment & Exits Diagram.

S E C T I O N   I V

O P E R A T I O N A L   E Q U I P M E N T

4-1. HEATING, VENTILATING AND PRESSURIZING EQUIPMENT.

  a. DESCRIPTION.

    (1) GENERAL.-Heat for cabin heating and defrosting is obtained from a Surface Combustion heater. Ventilation is obtained by operating the blower with the heater turned off. The turbosuperchargers supply air under pressure for cabin pressurization.

    (2) HEATING AND VENTILATING SYSTEM.-The controls for the heating system include the Heat Output knob, the Blower selective switch, the Blower Speed selective switch, the Heater Start push button, and the Cabin Air - Outside Air switch, all located on the cabin control panel (figure 23). The heater indicator light, adjacent to the heater push button, lights up when the heater shuts off. Cold air entry is controlled by opening or closing the "VENT" air control lever. (See figure 22.)

    (3) OPERATING INSTRUCTIONS.

      (a) "BLOWER ONLY" - "BLOWER & HEATER" switch - "BLOWER ONLY" position for ventilation. "BLOWER & HEATER" position for heat.

      (b) Heater "START" button - push only when "BLOWER & HEATER" above is selected. Hold button until heater is in operation as indicated by heater light going off.

      (c) Blower Speed switch - "LOW", "MED LOW", "MED HIGH", or "HIGH" position as required.

      (d) Heat Output knob - for heat, adjust to desired temperature as indicated on cabin temperature indicator (figure 25).

    (4) DEFROSTING EQUIPMENT.-The defrosters receive heated air by operation of the cabin heating system. The fuselage defrosting installations are as follows: six aspirating defrosters, located at the fuselage camera windows, one flexible defroster located at the transparent nose section,

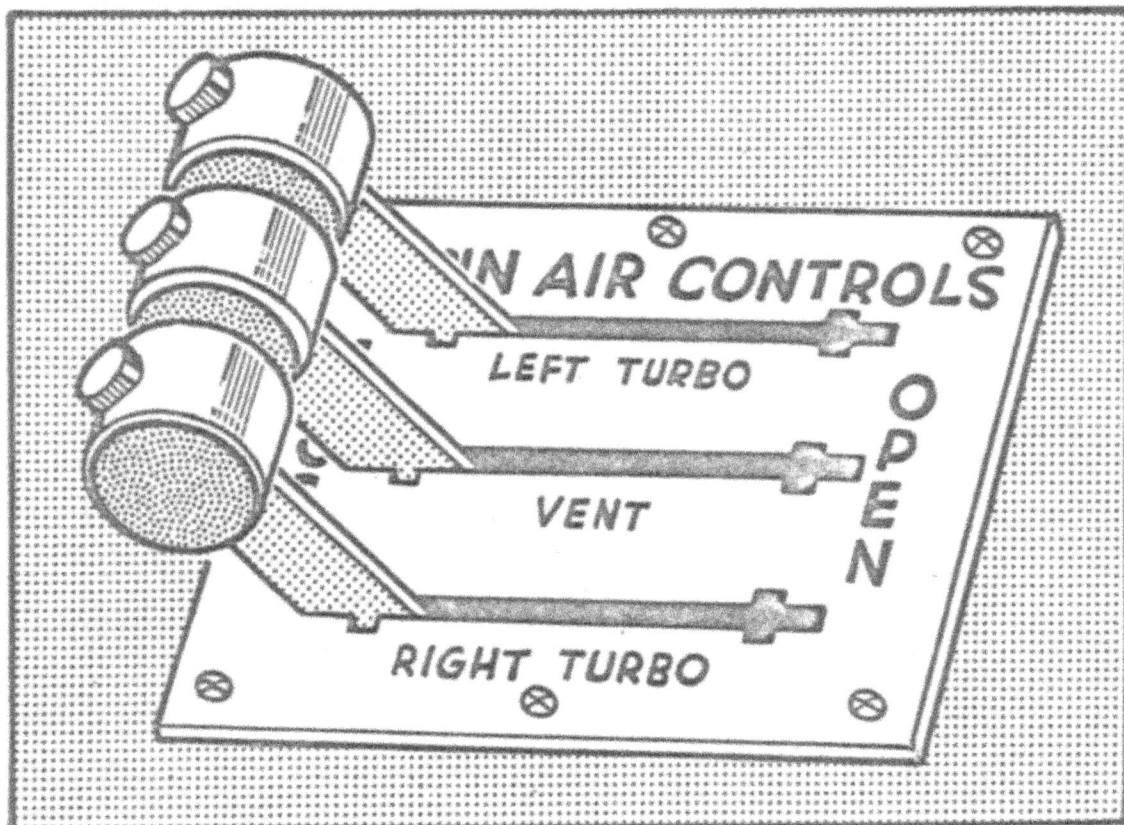

Figure 22 - Heat and Vent Controls.

three aspirating defrosters located in the pressurized canopy
section, and one defrosting shroud installed at the driftmeter.
The boom camera compartment is provided with a double defroster
for the two camera windows. Boom camera heat is controlled by
boom camera temperature regulator switch located on the cabin
air control panel (figure 23).

(a) BOOM CAMERA HEAT.-At start of flight, switch boom
camera temperature regulator switch to "AUTO-ON". (See figure
23.)

(b) DEFROSTING.

1. Heat and ventilating system - operating.

2. Canopy defrosters dampers - adjust as necessary.
Other defrosters are not controllable.

(5) PRESSURIZING SYSTEM.-Two turbosupercharger air flow
indicators, a cabin pressure altimeter, a "HIGH-LOW" cabin
pressure range switch, and an emergency shut-off horn button
are located on the cabin air control panel. (See figure 23.)
Two turbo manual override control levers (figures 6 and 22) are
located at the left-hand side of the pilot's seat and are marked
"OPEN" and "CLOSED". These levers are used to supply pressurized
air to the cabin and should be placed at "OPEN" at approximately
5000 feet altitude; at the same time the vent lever should be
placed at "CLOSED". In case of wing or nacelle fires, place in
"CLOSED" position. When carburetor heat is being applied the
respective turbo levers must be in the "CLOSED" position. (Ref.
Pg. 52 Section II-2-11-b and Warning.) A cabin pressure regulator
(20 figure 3) is mounted on the floor at the right side of the
pilot's station, and is calibrated to maintain cabin pressure
equal to 5000 feet altitude pressure at all altitudes from 5000
to 24,000 feet, and a 6.55 psi pressure differential above 24,000
feet altitude. A 2.75 psi pressure differential may be obtained
for combat use by moving the cabin pressure range switch to "LOW"
(figure 23), which actuates the pressure differential changing
device on the pressure regulator. A safety valve is located in
the cabin floor and connected to the nose wheel well. This valve
has three functions: first, as a pressure relief valve set to
open at 6.9 psi pressure differential; second, a vacuum relief
valve set to open upon existence of a cabin vacuum; third, a
cabin pressure dump valve which functions when the dump valve
lever (figure 23) is operated. Complete discharge of cabin
pressure can be made in 5 to 20 seconds. An automatic alarm
horn gives an intermittent tone when cabin altitude exceeds
12,000 feet altitude. The horn may be silenced by pressing the
horn shut-off button on the cabin air control panel.

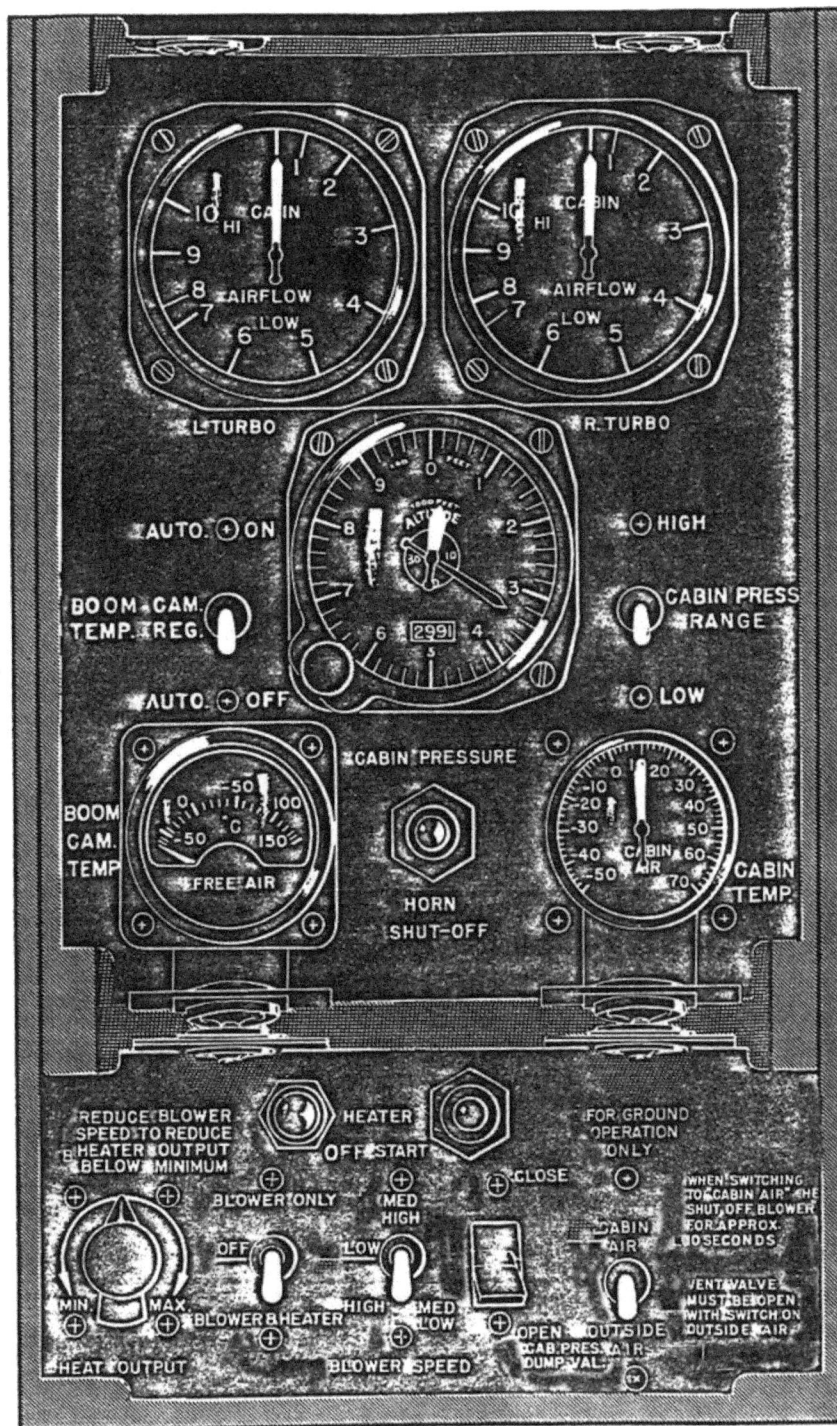

Figure 23 - Cabin Air Control.

(<u>a</u>) CABIN PRESSURIZING OPERATION.

<u>1</u>. Heat and ventilating system - operating.

(<u>b</u>) Cabin pressure dump valve lever - "CLOSE".

(<u>c</u>) Turbo levers - "OPEN".

(<u>d</u>) Vent lever - "CLOSED".

(<u>e</u>) Turbosuperchargers - operating at speed to produce desired low to high pressures as indicated on cabin airflow indicators. (See figure 23.)

(<u>f</u>) Cabin pressure range switch - "LOW" or "HIGH" to obtain desired cabin pressure differential.

(<u>g</u>) To depressurize immediately - move cabin pressure dump valve lever to "OPEN".

4-2. OXYGEN SYSTEM. (See figure 24.)

<u>a</u>. GENERAL.-The oxygen is supplied from four low pressure oxygen cylinders located aft of the left boom wheel well. Two cylinders supply only the pilot. The other two supply both the navigator's and photographer's stations, as well as the portable cylinder recharging outlet. Normal full pressure at the pilot's, navigator's and photographer's stations for the system is 400 psi which is released through three regulator units and three flow indicators. The oxygen cylinders may be refilled without removing them from the airplane by means of a filler valve located on the left side of the left boom. A walkaround type oxygen cylinder (figure 24) is located at the right side of the photographer's station. The walk-around cylinder recharger (figure 24) is at the right side of the photographer's station.

4-3. ARMAMENT.

<u>a</u>. BOMB RACKS.-One type S-1 electric bomb rack is installed under each wing to accommodate the 300 gallon fuel drop tanks. The release switch is on the pilot's fuel switch panel (figure 8). Bombs are not normally carried.

4-4. COMMUNICATION EQUIPMENT. (See figure 25.)

<u>a</u>. GENERAL.-The communications equipment consists of the following:

OXYGEN SYSTEM

Key to Figure 24.

1. Demand Mask to Regulator Tube

2. Flow Indicator

3. Pressure Gage

4. Check Valve

5. Demand Regulator

6. Type "D-2" Cylinder

7. Filler Access

8. Oxygen Cylinder Recharger

9. Portable Oxygen Cylinder

SUPPLY LINES
FILLER LINES

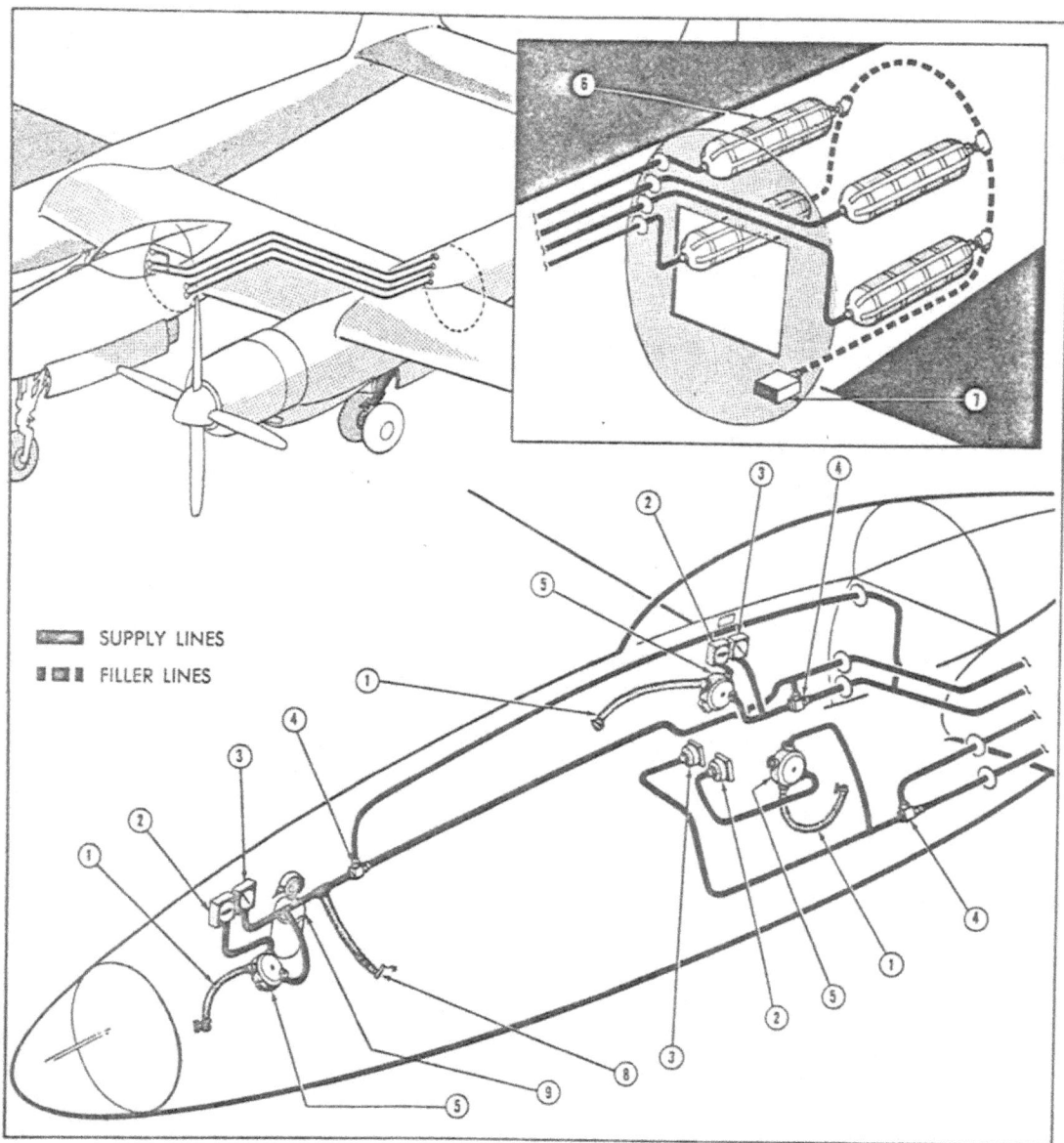

Figure 24 - Oxygen System.

Command Set, AN/ARC-3
Liaison Set, AN/ARC-8
Radio Compass, AN/ARN-7
Interphone Equipment, AN/AIC-2
Filter Equipment, RC-210
Marker Beacon Receiving Equipment, RC-193
Radio Set, SCR-695A
Radio Set, SCR-515-A (Alternate for SCR-695A)
Tail Warning, AN/APS-13
Radio Altimeter, SCR-718-A
Dinghy Radio Transmitter, SCR-578-B

All radio equipment, with the exception of the Dinghy, receives electrical power from the airplane's 24-volt dc power supply and 115-volt ac inverter.

b. COMMAND.-The AN/ARC-3 Command set may be controlled by either the pilot or navigator as the radio control panel (figure 26) is located on the fuselage wall at the right side of the pilot's seat and forward of the navigator's seat.

(1) OPERATION OF COMMAND SET AN/ARC-3.

(a) Insert headset plug in "TEL" (2 figure 26) and microphone plug in "MIC" (4 figure 26).

(b) Push any one of the eight channel-selector push buttons designated "A" through "H". This applies power to the equipment, which then automatically tunes to the frequency of the channel selected. Allow 30 to 45 seconds for the tubes in the equipment to reach normal operating temperature.

(c) To talk, press the microphone button (9 figure 15) on the throttle control handle.

(d) Release button to receive.

c. IDENTIFICATION.-The SCR-695 Identification set may be controlled by either crew member as the control switch is on the radio control panel. (See figure 26.)

(1) OPERATION OF IDENTIFICATION SET SCR-695.

(a) Move the "ON OFF" switch, (11 figure 26) located on the radio control panel to the "ON" position.

RADIO EQUIPMENT DIAGRAM

Key to Figure 25.

1. Radio Compass Antenna
2. Photographer's Jack Box
3. Radio Altimeter Indicator I-152-()
4. Radio Junction Box
5. Indicator Light APS-13
6. Radio Control Panel
7. Control Box ARN-7
8. Navigator's Jack Box
9. Inertia Switch
10. Marker Beacon Antenna
11. Marker Beacon Receiver
12. Receiver-Transmitter ARC-3
13. Receiver-Transmitter APS-13
14. Indicator Lamp Box BC-767
15. Power Junction Box Dynamotor ARC-3
16. Radio Receiver ARC-3
17. Radio Receiver BC-966-()
18. Radio Set SCR-578-B (Dinghy)
19. Indicator I-82-()
20. Monitor Switch (Liaison)
21. Remote Gain Control AIC-2
22. Liaison Receiver
23. Filter
24. Pilot's Jack Box
25. Code Key
26. Pilot's Mike Switch (throttle)
27. Marker Beacon Indicator Lamp
28. Indicator I-81-()
29. Dynamotor ART-13A
30. Radio Compass Receiver ARN-7
31. Transmitter ART-13
32. Interphone Amplifier AIC-2
33. Receiver-Transmitter BC-788
34. Radio Compass Sense Antenna
35. Radio Altimeter Antenna ARN-1
36. Antenna AN-95-C
37. R.H. Fin Tip Command Antenna
38. Liaison Antenna
39. Antenna System APS-13

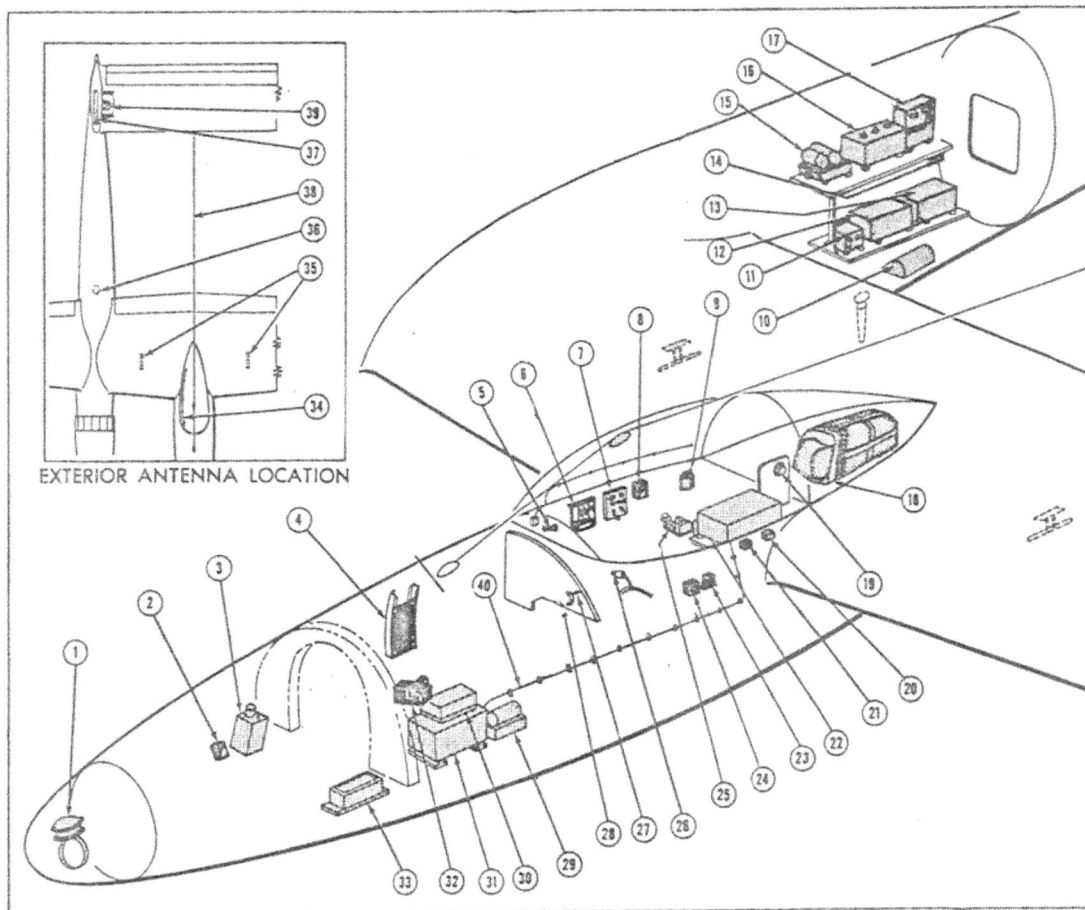

EXTERIOR ANTENNA LOCATION

Figure 25 - Radio Equipment Diagram.

(<u>b</u>) Set the six-position switch to the position desired.

d. LIAISON.-The Liaison set consists of the transmitter
T-47A/ART-13 (31 figure 25), located in the compartment passageway and the receiver BC-348-S (22 figure 25), located at the
navigator's station. The transmitter may be controlled by either
the pilot or navigator from the radio control panel switches
(figure 26). The receiver BC-348-S monitor switch (20 figure 25)
and liaison code key are located at the navigator's station and
controlled and operated by the navigator.

(1) OPERATION OF TRANSMITTER T-47A/ART-13.-To turn on the
liaison set, turn the transmitter selector switch (12 figure 26)
to the "VOICE" position.

CAUTION

Under no circumstances should the transmitter
be actually operating (key down or microphone
push-button closed) when the transmitter
selector switch is being operated. Such
operation, especially at high altitudes, can
cause an arc to occur.

(2) OPERATION OF RECEIVER BC-348-S.-Power to the receiver
is controlled by the "AVC-OFF-MVC" switch (10 figure 29). Plug
the headset into one of the jacks marked "TEL" and set the
receiver switch to "MVC" position.

e. INTERPHONE.-The AN/AIC-2 interphone equipment consists of
the amplifier AM-26/AIC (32 figure 25) located in the forward
compartment passageway, the remote gain control C-97/AIC-2 (21
figure 25) located above the navigator's table, and the BC-1366
jack boxes and equipment installed at each crew station. The
"ON-OFF" switch on the amplifier is normally safety wired in the
"ON" position and the system is controlled by the Master Battery
and Ignition Switch.

f. RADIO COMPASS.-The ARN-7 compass set (30 figure 25) is
located in the compartment passageway. The control switch is on
the radio compass control box (7 figure 25) and is accessible to
both pilot and navigator. The pilot's radio compass indicator
is located on the pilot's instrument panel (1 figure 7). An
indicator is also located on the navigator's instrument panel
(2 figure 29).

(1) OPERATION OF RADIO COMPASS ARN-7.-Move the function
switch (10 figure 4) to the "COMP", "ANT", or "LOOP" position,

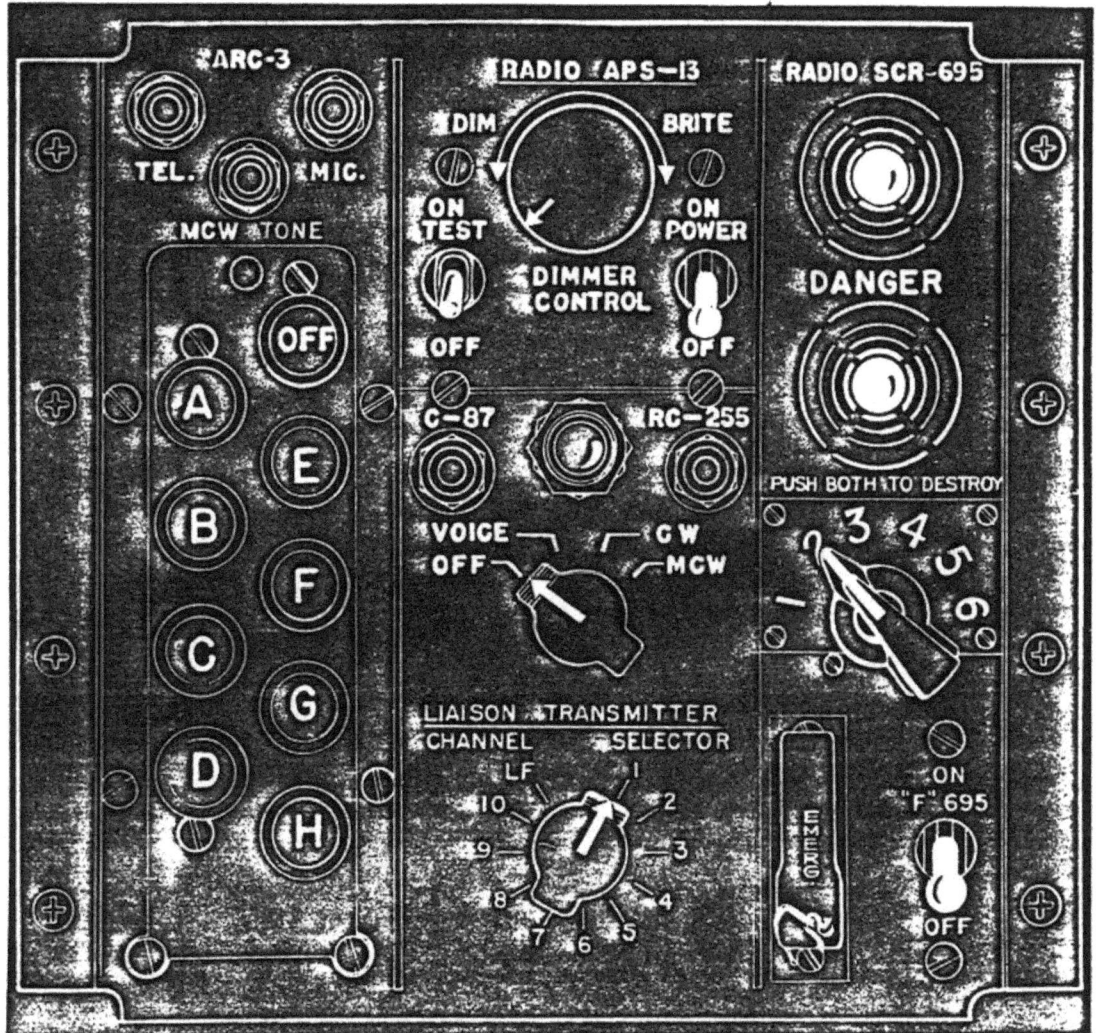

Figure 26 - Radio Control Panel.

and push in the "CONTROL" switch button. The green light will come on indicating the box has control of the equipment.

g. MARKER BEACON.-The BC-1333 marker beacon unit (28 figure 25) is installed in the right boom compartment. An indicator light (27 figure 25) is provided for the pilot only.

h. RADAR.-The APS-13 radar set is installed in the R.H. boom. An indicator light (5 figure 25) and warning bell (4A figure 4) are located at the pilot's station.

i. ALTIMETER.-The SCR-718 altimeter radio set, located at the photographer's station, includes Receiver-Transmitter BC-788 (33 figure 25) and an indicator (3 figure 25).

4-5. PHOTOGRAPHIC EQUIPMENT.

a. DESCRIPTION.

(1) GENERAL.-The following types of cameras may be installed in the fuselage and boom: (See figure 28).

(a) FUSELAGE.

Camera	Cone
K-17B	6-12-24-inch
K-18	24-inch
K-19A	12-inch
K-22	6-12-24-40-inch

(b) LEFT BOOM.

Camera	Cone
K-17	12-24-inch
K-18	24-inch
K-19A	12-inch
K-22	12-24-40-inch

(c) ADDITIONAL EQUIPMENT.

Hughes Type Automatic Camera Controls
Type B-3B Intervalometers
Type A-8 and A-11 Camera Mounts
Type A-2 Vertical View Finder
Ball Bank Sensitive Level Indicators
Vacuum Provision

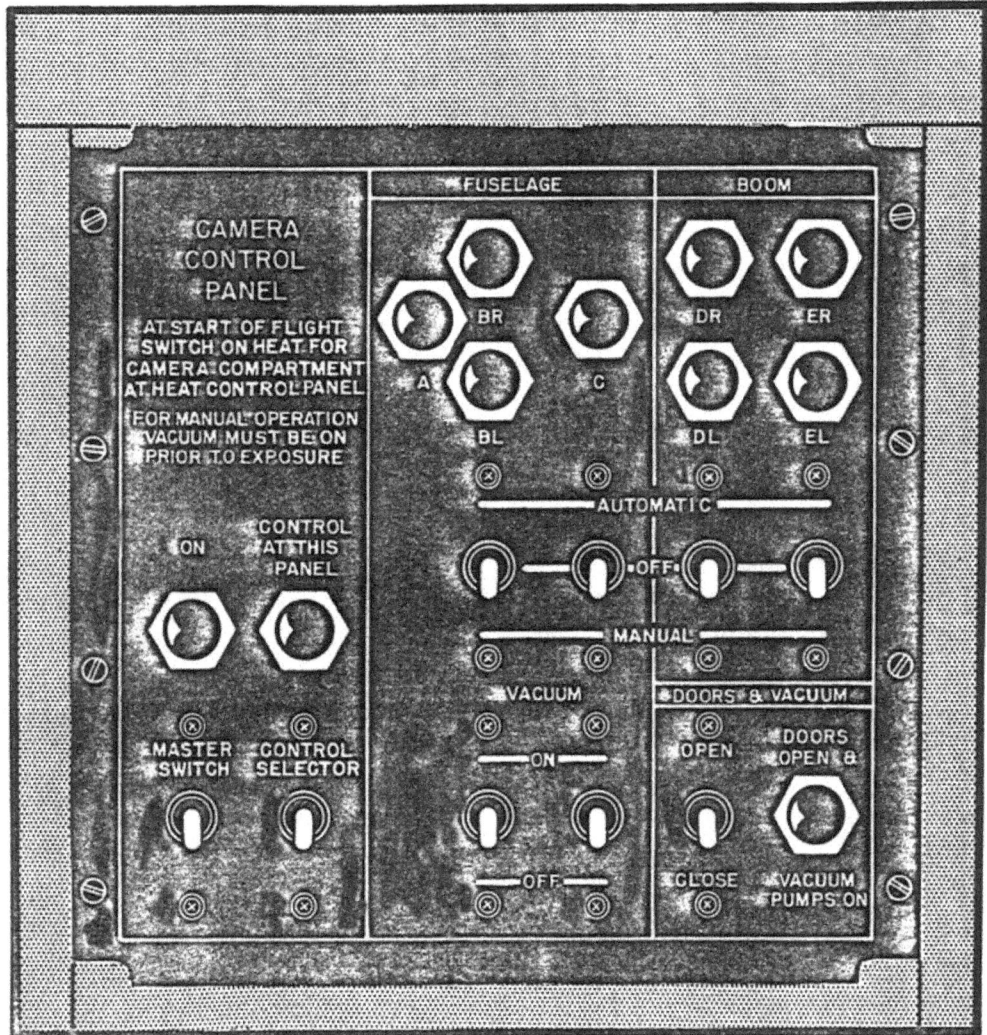

Figure 27 - Camera Control Panel.

(2) CONTROLS.

(a) GENERAL.-An automatic camera control is located on the right side of the photographer's compartment (3 figure 28).

b. OPERATION.

(1) GENERAL.-To operate the cameras, turn the master switch (figure 27) to the position that lights the indicator lamp directly above it, and turn the Control Selector switch to the position that lights the "Control at this Station" lamp. A separate switch is provided for electrical operation of the boom camera doors, and an indicator light (figure 27) will come on when the doors are fully "OPEN". The pilot must turn "ON" the electric heating switch (figure 23) for the boom camera compartment before each flight.

(2) MANUAL OPERATION. (See figure 27.)

(a) Master switch - Indicator Light ON.

(b) Control selector switch - Indicator Light ON.

(c) Vacuum switches - "ON".

(d) Boom camera switches "MANUAL".

(3) AUTOMATIC OPERATION. (See figures 27 and 28.)

(a) Intervalometer switch - "START".

(b) Master Switch - Indicator Light ON.

(c) Control Selector switch - Indicator Light ON.

(d) Vacuum switches - "ON".

(e) Boom camera doors switch - "OPEN".

(f) Camera switches - "AUTOMATIC".

NOTE

Indicator lights are provided for each camera and the vacuum system. (See figure 27.)

C A M E R A   E Q U I P M E N T   D I A G R A M

Key to Figure 28.

1.   Terminal Strip

2.   Relay Panel

3.   Photographer's Camera Control Panel

4.   K-17 or K-22 Cameras

5.   K-17, K-22, K-18, or K-19A Camera

6.   A-2 View Finder

7.   Photographer's Seat

8.   Vacuum Motors

9.   Intervalometers

10. Main Circuit Breaker Box

11. Pilot's Camera "ON" Warning Light

12. K-17, K-18, K-19A, or K-22 Cameras

13. Camera Door Actuator & Open Signal Switch

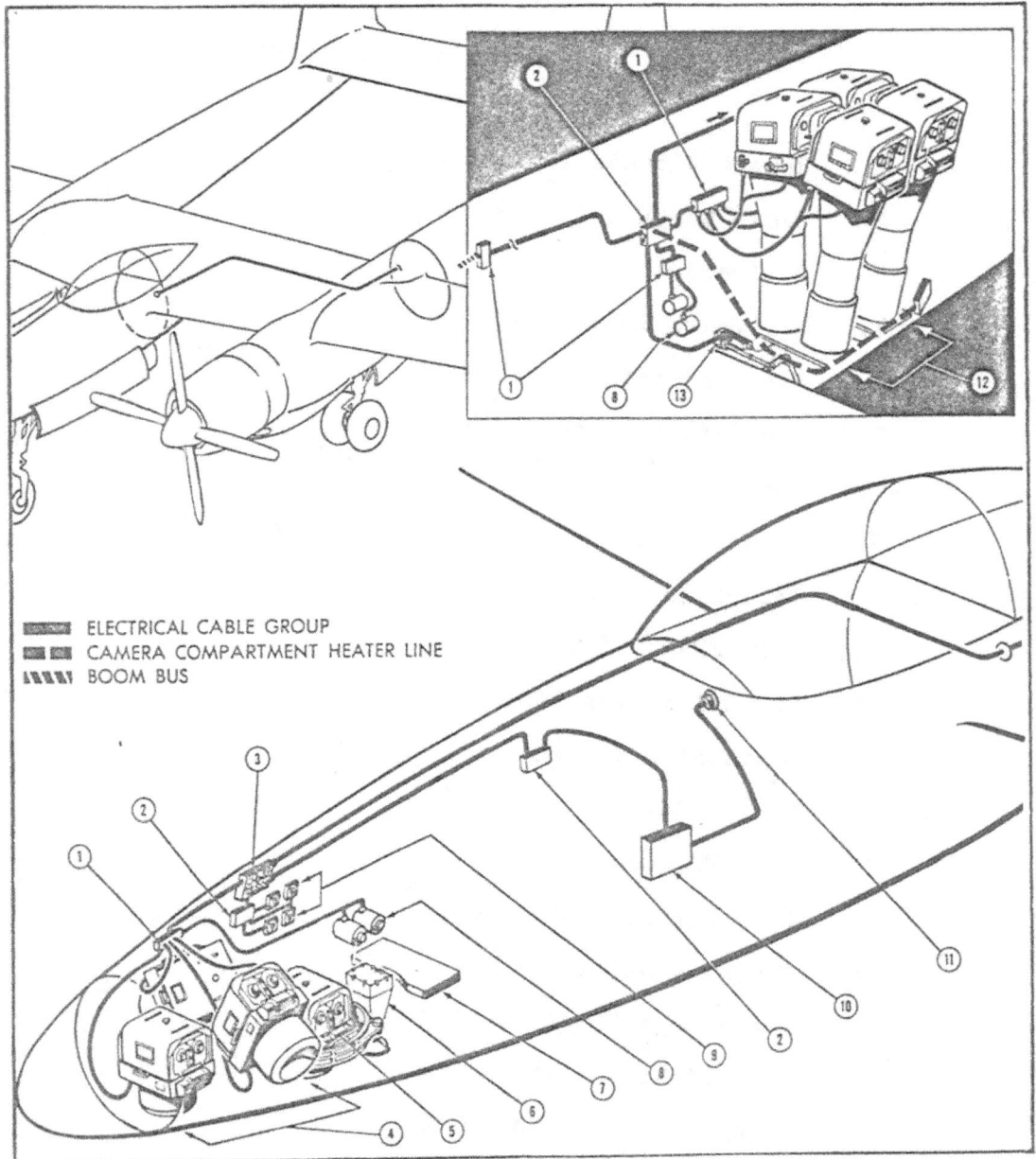

Figure 28 - Camera Equipment Diagram.

ELECTRICAL CABLE GROUP
CAMERA COMPARTMENT HEATER LINE
BOOM BUS

NAVIGATOR'S RADIO CONTROLS

Key to Figure 29.

1. Remote Compass Indicator

2. Radio Compass Indicator

3. Altimeter

4. Air Speed Indicator

5. Air Temperature Indicator

6. Air Position Indicator

7. Key

8. C. W. Oscillator

9. Telephone Jacks

10. AVC-OFF-MVC Switch

11. Crystal Filter Control

12. Monitoring Switch

13. Volume Control

14. Beat Frequency Control

15. Band Switch Control and Dial

16. Tuning Control

17. Interphone Remote Gain Control

18. Dial Light Rheostat

19. Antenna and Ground Posts

20. Antenna Alignment Control

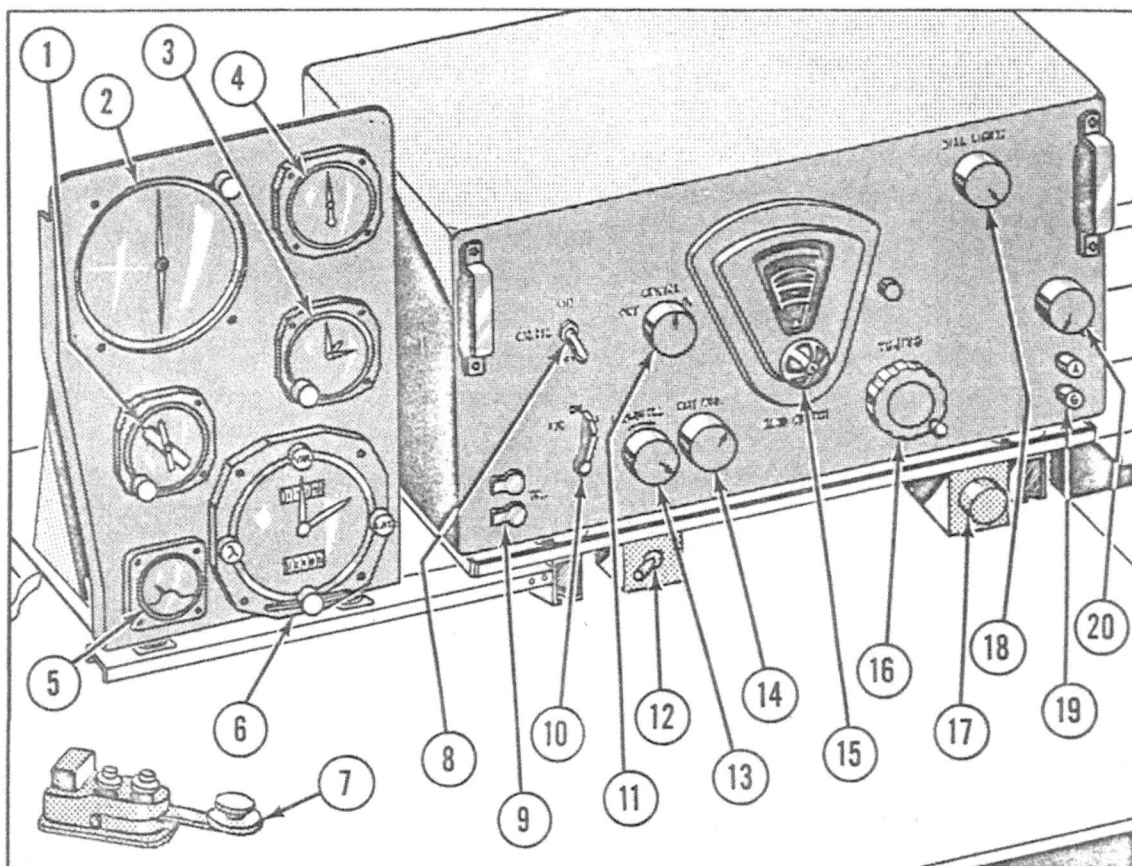

Figure 29 - Navigator's Radio Controls.

(g) To turn cameras off, the intervalometer switch (9 figure 28) and the switches on the camera control panel are placed in the "OFF" position.

4-6. NAVIGATOR'S COMPARTMENT.

a. NAVIGATION EQUIPMENT OPERATION.

(1) DRIFTMETER.-The driftmeter is operated by power supplied through the inverter switch (figure 8). A driftmeter master switch is located under the forward end of the liaison receiver. A defroster shroud supplies heat over the driftmeter from the cabin heating system.

b. ARMOR PLATE.-Provision has been made for armor plate protection at the pilot's and navigator's stations. (See figure 30.) The navigator's armor plate is fastened to the aft bulkhead at station 258. The upper plate may be turned inward and downward, thereby giving clearance to the aft releasable canopy if need for emergency egress occurs.

AIRPLANE ARMOR PROTECTS
PILOT AND NAVIGATOR FROM
ALL .30 CALIBER FIRE ORIGINATING
WITHIN THIS AREA.

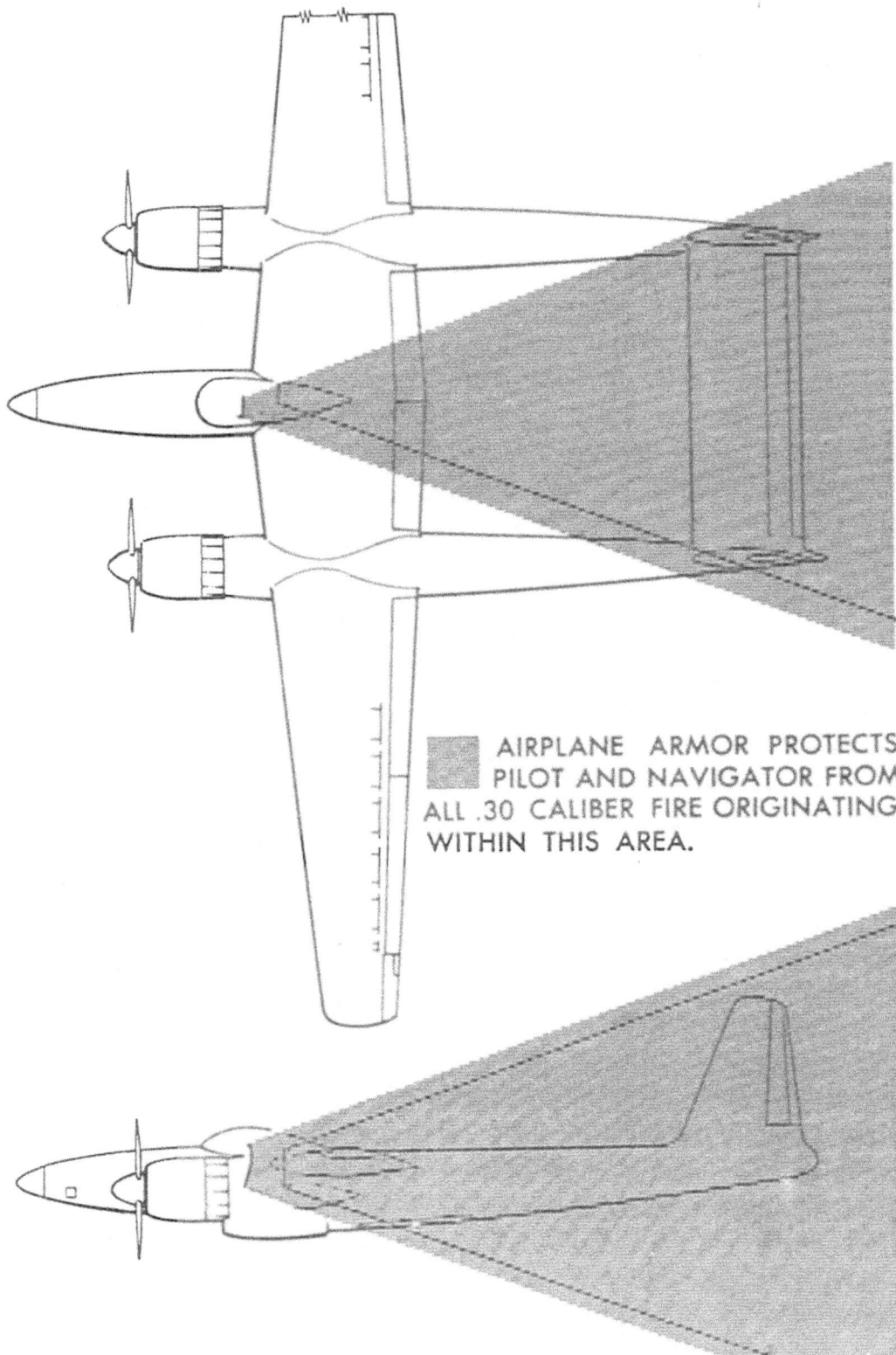

Figure 30 - Armor Protection Diagram.

A P P E N D I X   I.

1. FLIGHT PLANNING.

The following pages contain Instrument Range Markings and charts to be used as a guide to flight planning. Charts provided are a Take-off, Climb and Landing Chart, and a set of Flight Operation Instruction Charts for two-engine operation. The charts cover the probable gross weight range for the stated configuration.

An Airspeed Installation Correction Table, to be filled out by the Pilot when the information is available, is also included.

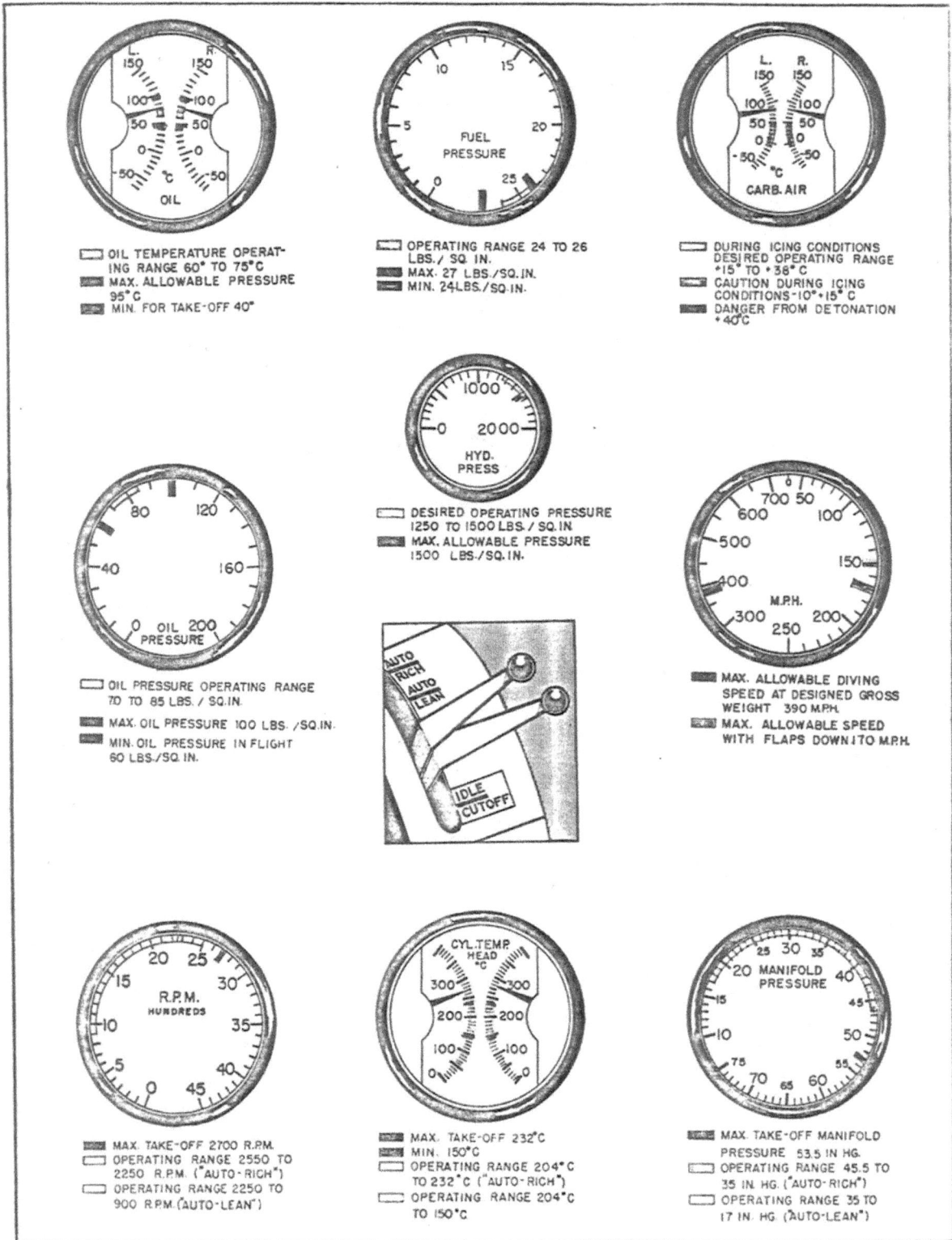

Figure 31 - Instrument Limitation Markings.

TAKE-OFF, CLIMB & LANDING CHART

AIRCRAFT MODEL(S): XF-11
ENGINE MODEL(S): R-4360-37

TAKE-OFF DISTANCE FEET

GROSS WEIGHT LB.	HEAD WIND M.P.H.	HEAD WIND KTS.	HARD SURFACE RUNWAY — AT SEA LEVEL GROUND RUN	TO CLEAR 50' OBJ.	AT 3000 FEET GROUND RUN	TO CLEAR 50' OBJ.	AT 6000 FEET GROUND RUN	TO CLEAR 50' OBJ.
60,000 Max.	0	0	2525	2940	2780	3230	3030	3530
	15	13.04	1950	2240	2160	2500	2350	2740
	30	26.05	1450	1690	1600	1860	1740	2030
	45	39.05	987	1205	1140	1325	1220	1450
47,500 Ave.	0	0	1440	1680	1580	1850	1730	2040
	15	13.04	1079	1260	1185	1390	1300	1530
	30	26.05	770	899	845	990	925	1090
	45	39.05	511	596	561	656	614	725
39,600 Min.	0	0	920	1119	1035	1230	1129	1340
	15	13.04	660	785	727	864	810	980
	30	26.05	461	548	507	603	530	656
	45	39.05	282	336	310	369	338	402

(SOD-TURF RUNWAY and SOFT SURFACE RUNWAY columns blank)

NOTE: INCREASE CHART DISTANCES AS FOLLOWS: 25% @ 10%; 100% @ 20%; 125% @ 30%; 150% @ 40%; 150% @ 40%

OPTIMUM TAKE-OFF WITH 2700 RPM, 53.5 In.Hg. & 20 DEG.FLAP IS 80% OF CHART VALUES

DATA AS OF 4-30-46   BASED ON: Estimated Performance

CLIMB DATA

GROSS WEIGHT LB.	AT SEA LEVEL BEST I.A.S. MPH	KTS	RATE OF CLIMB F.P.M.	GAL. FUEL USED	AT 5000 FEET BEST I.A.S. MPH	KTS	RATE OF CLIMB F.P.M.	FROM S.L. TIME MIN.	FUEL USED	AT 10,000 FEET BEST I.A.S. MPH	KTS	RATE OF CLIMB F.P.M.	FROM S.L. TIME MIN.	FUEL USED	AT 15,000 FEET BEST I.A.S. MPH	KTS	RATE OF CLIMB F.P.M.	FROM S.L. TIME MIN.	FUEL USED	AT 25,000 FEET BEST I.A.S. MPH	KTS	RATE OF CLIMB F.P.M.	FROM S.L. TIME MIN.	FUEL USED	AT 33,000 FEET BEST I.A.S. MPH	KTS	RATE OF CLIMB F.P.M.	FROM S.L. TIME MIN.	FUEL USED
60,000 Max.	170	148	1900	50	168	146	1850	2.5	65	156	136	1430	5.4	83	155	135	1350	8.9	100	152	132	1190	16.8	140	150	130	1000	24.0	176
47,500 Ave.	165	143	2610	50	164	142	2580	2.0	62	162	141	2540	4.0	75	159	130	1970	6.1	86	147	128	1810	11.4	113	145	126	1650	16.1	136
39,600 Min.	160	139	3300	50	159	138	3260	1.6	60	157	136	3210	3.0	68	155	135	3070	4.4	77	142	123	2300	8.2	97	140	121	2160	11.9	115

FUEL USED (U.S. GAL.) INCLUDES WARM-UP & TAKE-OFF ALLOWANCE

DATA AS OF 4-30-46   BASED ON: Estimated Performance

LANDING DISTANCE FEET

GROSS WEIGHT LB.	BEST IAS APPROACH POWER OFF MPH	KTS	POWER ON MPH	KTS	HARD DRY SURFACE — AT SEA LEVEL GROUND ROLL	TO CLEAR 50' OBJ.	AT 3000 FEET GROUND ROLL	TO CLEAR 50' OBJ.	AT 6000 FEET GROUND ROLL	TO CLEAR 50' OBJ.
60,000 Max.	114	99	107	93	2620	3600	2880	3890	3140	4160
47,500 Ave.	102	89	95	82	2070	2850	2280	3080	2490	3300
39,600 Min.	93	81	87	76	1730	2380	1900	2570	2070	2750

(FIRM DRY SOD and WET OR SLIPPERY columns blank)

DATA AS OF 4-30-46   BASED ON: Estimated Performance

OPTIMUM LANDING IS 80% OF CHART VALUES

LEGEND:
I.A.S. = INDICATED AIRSPEED
M.P.H. = MILES PER HOUR
KTS. = KNOTS
F.P.M. = FEET PER MINUTE

REMARKS: 50 Gal. fuel allowed for warm-up and take-off. Climb data based on full five minutes of military power operation followed by climb with normal rated power. Flap deflection 40° on landing.

NOTE: TO DETERMINE FUEL CONSUMPTION IN BRITISH IMPERIAL GALLONS, MULTIPLY BY 10, THEN DIVIDE BY 12.

CAUTION: ALL ABOVE DATA BASED ON ESTIMATED PERFORMANCE.

FIG.NO. 32   TAKE-OFF, CLIMB & LANDING CHART

FLIGHT OPERATION INSTRUCTION CHART

AIRCRAFT MODEL(S)
XF-11

ENGINE(S): R-4360-37

LIMITS	RPM.	M.P. IN.	BLOWER POSITION	MIXTURE POSITION	TIME LIMIT	CTL. TEMP.	TOTAL G.P.M.
WAR EMERG.			RATING NOT ESTABLISHED				
MILITARY POWER	2700	53.5	Turbo	A.R.	5 min.	232° C.	366

EXTERNAL LOAD ITEMS
DROP. FUEL TANKS

CHART WEIGHT LIMITS: 60,000 TO 50,000 POUNDS

NUMBER OF ENGINES OPERATING: Two (2)

NOTES: COLUMN I IS FOR EMERGENCY HIGH SPEED CRUISING ONLY. COLUMNS II,III,IV AND V GIVE PROGRESSIVE INCREASE IN RANGE AT A SACRIFICE IN SPEED. AIR MILES PER GALLON (MI./GAL.) (NO WIND), GALLONS PER HR. (G.P.H.) AND TRUE AIRSPEED (T.A.S.) ARE APPROXIMATE VALUES FOR REFERENCE. RANGE VALUES ARE FOR AN AVERAGE AIRPLANE FLYING ALONE (NO WIND). TO OBTAIN BRITISH IMPERIAL GAL. (OR G.P.H.): MULTIPLY U.S. GAL (OR G.P.H.) BY 10 THEN DIVIDE BY 12.

INSTRUCTIONS FOR USING CHART: SELECT FIGURE IN FUEL COLUMN EQUAL TO OR LESS THAN AMOUNT OF FUEL TO BE USED FOR CRUISING MOVE HORIZONTALLY TO RIGHT OR LEFT AND SELECT RANGE VALUE EQUAL TO OR GREATER THAN THE STATUTE OR NAUTICAL AIR MILES TO BE FLOWN. VERTICALLY BELOW AND OPPOSITE VALUE NEAREST DESIRED CRUISING ALTITUDE (ALT.) READ RPM, MANIFOLD PRESSURE (M.P.) AND MIXTURE SETTING REQUIRED.

COLUMN I

RANGE IN AIRMILES		FUEL
STATUTE	NAUTICAL	U.S. GAL.
1155	1000	2705
1135	985	2640
1045	910	2600
960	835	2400
875	760	2200
770	685	2000
700	610	1800
610	530	1600
		1400

FROM POWER PLANT CHART FOR DETAILS SEE (FIG. 22 SECT. III)

MAXIMUM CONTINUOUS

PRESS. ALT. FEET	R.P.M.	M.P. INCHES	MIX- TURE	TOT. GPH	APPROX. T.A.S. MPH	KTS.
40000				392		
35000				377		
30000				360		
25000	2550	46.5	A.R.	600	407	353
20000						
15000						
10000				342		
5000				325		
S.L.	2550	46.5	A.R.	690	308	267

COLUMN II

RANGE IN AIRMILES		FUEL
STATUTE	NAUTICAL	U.S. GAL.

(STAT. (NAUT.) MI./GAL.)

PRESS. ALT. FEET	R.P.M.	M.P. INCHES	MIX- TURE	TOT. GPH	APPROX. T.A.S. MPH	KTS.

COLUMN III

RANGE IN AIRMILES		FUEL
STATUTE	NAUTICAL	U.S. GAL.
SUBTRACT FUEL ALLOWANCES NOT AVAILABLE FOR CRUISING	2045	2640
	2015	2600
1775		2400
1750		2200
1860	1615	2000
1710	1495	1800
1550	1345	1600
1395	1210	1400
1220	1075	
1085	940	

CALCULATED DATA

(STAT. (.789 NAUT.) MI./GAL.)

PRESS. ALT. FEET	R.P.M.	M.P. INCHES	MIX- TURE	TOT. GPH	APPROX. T.A.S. MPH	KTS.
40000				294	341	307
35000					328	296
30000	2230	36.0	A.L.		313	285
						272
25000						
20000						
15000					298	259
10000					283	245
5000	2230	36.0	A.L.	294	268	232
S.L.						

COLUMN IV

RANGE IN AIRMILES		FUEL
STATUTE	NAUTICAL	U.S. GAL.

(NAUT.) MI./GAL.)

PRESS. ALT. FEET	R.P.M.	M.P. INCHES	MIX- TURE	TOT. GPH	APPROX. T.A.S. MPH	KTS.

COLUMN V

RANGE IN AIRMILES		FUEL
STATUTE	NAUTICAL	U.S. GAL.
3470	3015	2640
3420	2970	2600
3155	2740	2400
2890	2510	2200
2630	2285	2000
2365	2055	1800
2100	1825	1600
1840	1595	1400

MAXIMUM AIR RANGE

PRESS. ALT. FEET	R.P.M.	M.P. INCHES	MIX- TURE	TOT. GPH	APPROX. T.A.S. MPH	KTS.
40000				204	305	265
35000	1850	36.0	A.L.		283	247
30000				193	256	222
25000	1650	35.0		167	235	204
20000	1550	35.0		154		
15000	1450	35.0				
10000	1350	35.0		141	218	189
5000	1250	35.0		131	204	176
S.L.	1200	31.0	A.L.	121	187	162

EXAMPLE

AT 57,000 LB. GROSS WEIGHT WITH 2400 GAL. OF FUEL (AFTER DEDUCTING TOTAL ALLOWANCES OF 64 GAL.) TO FLY 1860 STAT. AIRMILES AT 5,000 FT. ALTITUDE MAINTAIN 2230 RPM AND 36.0 IN. MANIFOLD PRESSURE WITH MIXTURE SET: Automatic Lean

SPECIAL NOTES

(1) MAKE ALLOWANCE FOR WARM-UP, TAKE-OFF & CLIMB (SEE FIG. 32) PLUS ALLOWANCE FOR WIND, RESERVE AND COMBAT AS REQUIRED.

(2) Column explanation:
  I. Normal rated power operation.
  III. Maximum cruise operation (1675 BHP)
  V. Maximum range.

LEGEND

ALT. : PRESSURE ALTITUDE	F.R. : FULL RICH
M.P. : MANIFOLD PRESSURE	A.R. : AUTO-RICH
GPH : U.S. GAL. PER HOUR	A.L. : AUTO-LEAN
TAS : TRUE AIRSPEED	C.L. : CRUISING LEAN
KTS. : KNOTS	M.L. : MANUAL LEAN
S.L. : SEA LEVEL	F.T. : FULL THROTTLE

DATA AS OF 4-30-46   BASED ON: Estimated Data

RED FIGURES ARE PRELIMINARY DATA, SUBJECT TO REVISION AFTER FLIGHT CHECK

FIG. NO. 33   FLIGHT OPERATING INSTRUCTION CHART (SHEET 1 OF 2 SHEETS)

FLIGHT OPERATION INSTRUCTION CHART

AIRCRAFT MODEL(S)
XF-11

ENGINE(S): R-4360-C-5?

LIMITS	RPM	M.P. IN.HG.	BLOWER POSITION	MIXTURE POSITION	TIME LIMIT	CYL. TEMP.	TOTAL G.P.H.
WAR EMERG.		RATING NOT ESTABLISHED					
MILITARY	2700	53.5	Turbo	A.R.	5 min.	232° C.	366

FOR DETAILS SEE POWER PLANT CHART (FIG 20 SECT.III)

CHART WEIGHT LIMITS: 50,000 TO 40,000 POUNDS

EXTERNAL LOAD ITEMS

DROP. FUEL TANKS

NUMBER OF ENGINES OPERATING: TWO (2)

INSTRUCTIONS FOR USING CHART: SELECT FIGURE IN FUEL COLUMN EQUAL TO OR LESS THAN AMOUNT OF FUEL TO BE USED FOR CRUISING. MOVE HORIZONTALLY TO RIGHT OR LEFT AND SELECT RANGE VALUE EQUAL TO OR GREATER THAN THE STATUTE OR NAUTICAL AIR MILES TO BE FLOWN. VERTICALLY BELOW AND OPPOSITE VALUE NEAREST DESIRED CRUISING ALTITUDE (ALT.) READ RPM, MANIFOLD PRESSURE (M.P.) AND MIXTURE SETTING REQUIRED.

NOTES: COLUMN I IS FOR EMERGENCY HIGH SPEED CRUISING ONLY. COLUMNS II, III, IV AND V GIVE PROGRESSIVE INCREASE IN RANGE AT A SACRIFICE IN SPEED. AIR MILES PER GALLON (MI./GAL.) (NO WIND), GALLONS PER HR. (G.P.H.) AND TRUE AIRSPEED (T.A.S.) ARE APPROXIMATE VALUES FOR REFERENCE. RANGE VALUES ARE FOR AN AVERAGE AIRPLANE FLYING ALONE (NO WIND). TO OBTAIN BRITISH IMPERIAL GAL (OR G.P.H.) MULTIPLY U.S. GAL. (OR G.P.H.) BY 10 THEN DIVIDE BY 12.

COLUMN I

RANGE IN AIRMILES		FUEL	MAXIMUM CONTINUOUS					
STATUTE	NAUTICAL	U.S. GAL.						
615	535	1400						
525	455	1200						
435	380	1000						
350	305	800						
265	230	600						
175	150	400						
90	75	200						
45	40	100						

MAXIMUM CONTINUOUS

PRESS ALT. FEET	M.P. INCHES	R.P.M.	MIX- TURE	TOT. GPM	APPROX. MPH	T.A.S. KTS.
40000						
35000						
30000	46.5	600	A.R.		419	364
25000					402	348
20000					383	332
15000					365	317
10000					347	301
5000					328	285
S.L.	46.5	600	A.R.		309	268

(bottom) 2550 46.5 600 A.R.

COLUMN II

RANGE IN AIRMILES		FUEL		
STATUTE	NAUTICAL			

COLUMN III

RANGE IN AIRMILES			
STATUTE	NAUTICAL		
1105	960		
945	820		
790	685		
630	545		
475	410		
315	275		
160	140		
80	70		

SUBTRACT FUEL ALLOWANCES NOT AVAILABLE FOR CRUISING

(.928 STAT.) (.806 NAUT.) MI./GAL.

PRESS ALT. FEET	M.P. INCHES	R.P.M.	MIX- TURE	TOT. GPM	APPROX. MPH	T.A.S. KTS.
40000						
35000						
30000	36.0	2230	A.L.	294	370	321
25000					355	308
20000					338	293
15000					322	279
10000					306	265
5000					290	252
S.L.	36.0	2230	A.L.	294	273	237

COLUMN IV

RANGE IN AIRMILES			
STATUTE	NAUTICAL		

CALCULATED DATA

(NAUT.) MI./GAL.

STAT. ( ) MI./GAL.

COLUMN V

RANGE IN AIRMILES		FUEL	MAXIMUM AIR RANGE					
STATUTE	NAUTICAL	U.S. GAL.						
2220	1925	1400						
1905	1655	1200						
1590	1380	1000						
1270	1105	800						
950	825	600						
635	550	400						
320	280	200						
160	140	100						

MAXIMUM AIR RANGE

PRESS ALT. FEET	M.P. INCHES	R.P.M.	MIX- TURE	TOT. GPM	APPROX. MPH	T.A.S. KTS.
40000						
35000						
30000	34.5	1400	A.L.	137	273	237
25000	34.0	1300		134	249	216
20000	34.0	1225		123	230	200
15000	35.0	1150		113	211	18?
10000	36.0	1075		103	19?	170
5000	38.0	1000		96	180	156
S.L.	37.0	1000	A.L.	90	168	146

SPECIAL NOTES

(1) MAKE ALLOWANCE FOR WARM-UP, TAKE-OFF & CLIMB (SEE FIG. 32) PLUS ALLOWANCE FOR WIND, RESERVE AND COMBAT AS REQUIRED.

(2) Column explanation:
　I. Normal rated power operation.
　III. Maximum cruise operation (1675 BHP).
　V. Maximum range.

EXAMPLE

AT 48,000 LB. GROSS WEIGHT WITH 1000 GAL. OF FUEL (AFTER DEDUCTING TOTAL ALLOWANCES OF 62 GAL.) TO FLY 790 STAT. AIRMILES AT 5,000 FT. ALTITUDE MAINTAIN 2230 RPM AND 36.0 IN. MANIFOLD PRESSURE WITH MIXTURE SET: Automatic Lean

LEGEND

ALT. : PRESSURE ALTITUDE
M.P. : MANIFOLD PRESSURE
GPH : U.S. GAL. PER HOUR
IAS : TRUE AIRSPEED
KTS. : KNOTS
S.L. : SEA LEVEL

F.R. : FULL RICH
A.R. : AUTO-RICH
A.L. : AUTO-LEAN
C.L. : CRUISING LEAN
M.L. : MANUAL LEAN
F.T. : FULL THROTTLE

DATA AS OF 4-30-46　BASED ON: Estimated Data

RED FIGURES ARE PRELIMINARY DATA, SUBJECT TO REVISION AFTER FLIGHT CHECK

FLIGHT OPERATION INSTRUCTION CHART

AIRCRAFT MODEL(S): XF-11

ENGINE(S): R-4360-37

EXTERNAL LOAD ITEMS: DROP. FUEL TANKS

NUMBER OF ENGINES OPERATING: ONE (1)

CHART WEIGHT LIMITS: 60,000 TO 50,000 POUNDS

LIMITS	RPM	M.P. IN. HG.	BLOWER POSITION	MIXTURE POSITION	TIME LIMIT	CYL. TEMP.	TOTAL G.P.M.
WAR EMERG.				RATING NOT ESTABLISHED			
MILITARY POWER	2700	53.5	Turbo	A.R.	5 min.	232° C.	366

NOTES: COLUMN I IS FOR EMERGENCY HIGH SPEED CRUISING ONLY. COLUMNS II,III,IV AND V GIVE PROGRESSIVE INCREASE IN RANGE AT A SACRIFICE IN SPEED. AIR MILES PER GALLON (MI./GAL.)(NO WIND), GALLONS PER HR. (G.P.H.) AND TRUE AIRSPEED (T.A.S.) ARE APPROXIMATE VALUES FOR REFERENCE. RANGE VALUES ARE FOR AN AVERAGE AIRPLANE FLYING ALONE (NO WIND). TO OBTAIN BRITISH IMPERIAL GAL. (OR G.P.H.) MULTIPLY U.S. GAL. (OR G.P.H.) BY 10 THEN DIVIDE BY 12.

INSTRUCTIONS FOR USING CHART: SELECT FIGURE IN FUEL COLUMN EQUAL TO OR LESS THAN AMOUNT OF FUEL TO BE USED FOR CRUISING. MOVE HORIZONTALLY TO RIGHT OR LEFT AND SELECT RANGE VALUE EQUAL TO OR GREATER THAN THE STATUTE OR NAUTICAL AIR MILES TO BE FLOWN. VERTICALLY BELOW AND OPPOSITE VALUE NEAREST DESIRED CRUISING ALTITUDE (ALT.) READ RPM, MANIFOLD PRESSURE (M.P.) AND MIXTURE SETTING REQUIRED.

(CALCULATED DATA)

COLUMN I

FUEL U.S. GAL.	RANGE IN AIRMILES STATUTE	NAUTICAL
2705	1700	1475
2640	1675	1455
2600		
2400	1545	1340
2200	1415	1230
2000	1285	1115
1800	1160	1010
1600	1030	895
1400	900	780

MAXIMUM CONTINUOUS

PRESS ALT. FEET	R.P.M.	M.P. INCHES	MIX-TURE	TOT. GPM	MPH	KTS.
40000						
35000						
30000	2550	46.5	A.R.	300	255	222
25000					252	219
20000					250	217
15000					246	214
10000					212	210
5000					234	203
S.L.	2550	46.5	A.R.	300	227	197

COLUMN III

FUEL U.S. GAL.	RANGE IN AIRMILES STATUTE	NAUTICAL
	3020	2625
	2975	2585
	2745	2385
	2520	2190
	2290	1990
	2060	1790
	1830	1590
	1600	1390

FUEL ALLOWANCES NOT AVAILABLE FOR CRUISING

PRESS ALT. FEET	R.P.M.	M.P. INCHES	MIX-TURE	TOT. GPM	MPH	KTS.
40000						
35000						
30000	2230	36.0	A.L.	147	222	193
25000					219	190
20000					218	189
15000					214	186
10000					210	182
5000					204	177
S.L.	2230	36.0	A.L.	147	198	172

MAXIMUM AIR RANGE

EXAMPLE

A 57,000 LB. CROSS WEIGHT WITH 2400 GAL. OF FUEL (AFTER DEDUCTING TOTAL ALLOWANCES OF 64 GAL.) TO FLY 2745 STAT. AIR MILES AT 5,000' T. ALTITUDE MAINTAIN 2230 RPM AND 36.0 IN. MANIFOLD PRESSURE WITH MIXTURE SET: Automatic Lean

SPECIAL NOTES

(1) MAKE ALLOWANCE FOR WARM-UP, TAKE-OFF & CLIMB (SEE FIG. 32) PLUS ALLOWANCE FOR WIND, RESERVE AND COMBAT AS REQUIRED.
(2) Column Explanation:
I. Normal rated power operation.
III. Maximum cruise operation (1675 BHP).

LEGEND

ALT.: PRESSURE ALTITUDE
M.P.: MANIFOLD PRESSURE
GPM: U.S.GAL.PER HOUR
TAS: TRUE AIRSPEED
KTS.: KNOTS
S.L.: SEA LEVEL

F.R.: FULL RICH
A.R.: AUTO-RICH
A.L.: AUTO-LEAN
C.L.: CRUISING LEAN
M.L.: MANUAL LEAN
F.T.: FULL THROTTLE

RED FIGURES ARE PRELIMINARY DATA, SUBJECT TO REVISION AFTER FLIGHT CHECK

DATA AS OF 4-30-46 BASED ON: Estimated Data

FLIGHT OPERATION INSTRUCTION CHART

AIRCRAFT MODEL(S)

XP-11

ENGINE(S): R-4360-37

LIMITS	M.P. IN.HG.	BLOWER POSITION	MIXTURE POSITION	TIME LIMIT	CYL. TEMP.	TOTAL G.P.M.
	RPM					
WAR EMERG.		RATING NOT ESTABLISHED				
MILITARY POWER	2700	53.5	Turbo	A.R.	5 min.	2320 C. 366

FOR DETAILS SEE POWER PLANT CHART (FIG.20 SECT.III)

EXTERNAL LOAD ITEMS

DROP. FUEL TANKS

NUMBER OF ENGINES OPERATING: ONE (1)

CHART WEIGHT LIMITS: 50,000 TO 40,000 POUNDS

INSTRUCTIONS FOR USING CHART: SELECT FIGURE IN FUEL COLUMN EQUAL TO OR LESS THAN AMOUNT OF FUEL TO BE USED FOR CRUISING. MOVE HORIZONTALLY TO RIGHT OR LEFT AND SELECT RANGE VALUE EQUAL TO OR GREATER THAN THE STATUTE OR NAUTICAL AIR MILES TO BE FLOWN. VERTICALLY BELOW AND OPPOSITE VALUE NEAREST DESIRED CRUISING ALTITUDE (ALT.) READ RPM, MANIFOLD PRESSURE (M.P.) AND MIXTURE SETTING REQUIRED.

NOTES: COLUMN I IS FOR EMERGENCY HIGH SPEED CRUISING ONLY. COLUMNS II,III,IV AND V GIVE PROGRESSIVE INCREASE IN RANGE AT A SACRIFICE IN SPEED. AIR MILES PER GALLON (MI./GAL.)(NO WIND),GALLONS PER HR. (G.P.H.) AND TRUE AIRSPEED (T.A.S.) ARE APPROXIMATE VALUES FOR REFERENCE. RANGE VALUES ARE FOR AN AVERAGE AIRPLANE FLYING ALONE (NO WIND). TO OBTAIN BRITISH IMPERIAL GAL.(OR G.P.H.):MULTIPLY U.S.GAL.(OR G.P.H.) BY 10 THEN DIVIDE BY 12.

COLUMN I

RANGE IN AIRMILES		FUEL
STATUTE	NAUTICAL	U.S. GAL.
937	815	1400
800	695	1200
670	580	1000
535	465	800
400	350	600
270	235	400
135	115	200
65	55	130

MAXIMUM CONTINUOUS

(STAT. (MI./GAL.)) (NAUT.) MI./GAL.)

R.P.M.	M.P. INCHES	MIX-TURE	TOT. G.P.H.	T.A.S. MPH	T.A.S. KTS.	PRESS ALT. FEET
		A.R.	300	292 254		40000 / 35000 / 30000
				286 248 / 283 243 / 271 235		25000 / 20000 / 15000
2550	46.5	A.R.	300	265 227 / 249 216 / 236 205		10000 / 5000 / S.L.
2550	46.5					

COLUMN II

RANGE IN AIRMILES		
STATUTE	NAUTICAL	

SUBTRACT FUEL ALLOWANCES NOT AVAILABLE FOR CRUISING [1]

(STAT. (MI./GAL.)) (NAUT.) MI./GAL.)

R.P.M.	M.P. INCHES	MIX-TURE	TOT. G.P.H.	T.A.S. MPH	T.A.S. KTS.	PRESS ALT. FEET

COLUMN III

RANGE IN AIRMILES	
STATUTE	NAUTICAL
1670	1453
1240	1240
1190	1035
955	830
715	620
475	410
240	210
120	105

(STAT. (121 STAT.) MI./GAL.) (1.402 NAUT.(1.215NAUT.) MI./GAL.)

R.P.M.	M.P. INCHES	MIX-TURE	TOT. G.P.H.	T.A.S. MPH	T.A.S. KTS.
		A.L.	147	255	221
				249 216 / 244 212 / 236 205	
2230	36.0				
2230	36.0	A.L.	147	228 198 / 217 188 / 206 179	

COLUMN IV

RANGE IN AIRMILES		FUEL
STATUTE	NAUTICAL	U.S. GAL.

(STAT. (MI./GAL.)) (NAUT.) MI./GAL.)

R.P.M.	M.P. INCHES	MIX-TURE	TOT. G.P.H.	T.A.S. MPH	T.A.S. KTS.	PRESS ALT. FEET

COLUMN V

RANGE IN AIRMILES	
STATUTE	NAUTICAL

MAXIMUM AIR RANGE

A.P.M.	M.P. INCHES	MIX-TURE	TOT. G.P.H.	T.A.S. MPH	T.A.S. KTS.	PRESS ALT. FEET
						40000 / 35000 / 30000
						25000 / 20000 / 15000
						10000 / 5000 / S.L.

(Rotated watermark:) CALCULATED DATA

SPECIAL NOTES

(1) MAKE ALLOWANCE FOR WARM-UP,TAKE-OFF & CLIMB (SEE FIG.32) PLUS ALLOWANCE FOR WIND,RESERVE AND COMBAT AS REQUIRED.

(2) Column explanation:
  I. Normal rated power operation.
  II. Maximum cruise operation.
  III. Maximum cruise operation

EXAMPLE

AT 48,000LB.GROSS WEIGHT WITH 1000 GAL.OF FUEL (AFTER DEDUCTING TOTAL ALLOWANCES OF 62 GAL.) TO FLY 1190 STAT.AIRMILES AT 5,000FT.ALTITUDE MAINTAIN 2230 RPM AND 36.0IN.MANIFOLD PRESSURE WITH MIXTURE SET: Automatic Lean

LEGEND

ALT. : PRESSURE ALTITUDE	F.R. : FULL RICH	
M.P. : MANIFOLD PRESSURE	A.R. : AUTO-RICH	
GPM : U.S.GAL.PER HOUR	A.L. : AUTO-LEAN	
TAS : TRUE AIRSPEED	C.L. : CRUISING LEAN	
KTS. : KNOTS	M.L. : MANUAL LEAN	
S.L. : SEA LEVEL	F.T. : FULL THROTTLE	

DATA AS OF 6-30-46   BASED ON: Estimated Data

RED FIGURES ARE PRELIMINARY DATA,SUBJECT TO REVISION AFTER FLIGHT CHECK

FIG. NO. 34   FLIGHT OPERATING INSTRUCTION CHART (SHEET 2 OF 2 SHEETS)

S E C T I O N   IV.

F L I G H T   O P E R A T I N G   D A T A

AIRSPEED INSTALLATION CORRECTION TABLE

I. A. S.	CORRECTION
Flaps and Gears Retracted	
100 Miles	
200 Miles	
250 Miles	
300 Miles	
350 Miles	
Flaps and Gears Extended	
74 Miles	
80 Miles	
90 Miles	
100 Miles	
110 Miles	
140 Miles	
150 Miles	

To be filled out by the pilot
when information is available.

RESTRICTED

SPRUCE GOOSE

HUGHES FLYING BOAT MANUAL

~~RESTRICTED~~

Originally Published by the War Department
Reprinted by Periscope Film LLC

NOW AVAILABLE!

WARSHIPS DVD SERIES

WARSHIPS: CARRIER MISHAPS

AIRCRAFT CARRIER
MISHAPS
SAFETY AND TRAINING FILMS

-PERISCOPEFILM.COM-

DVD

NOW AVAILABLE ON DVD!

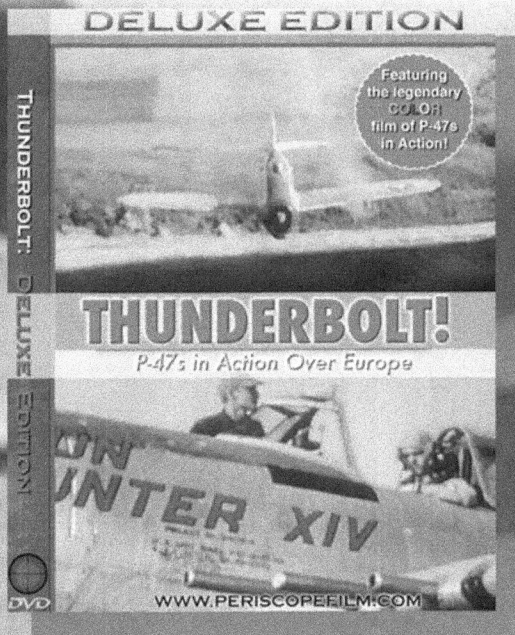

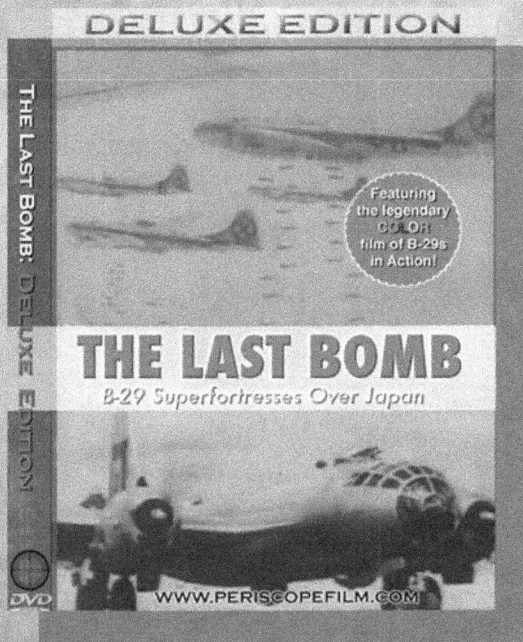

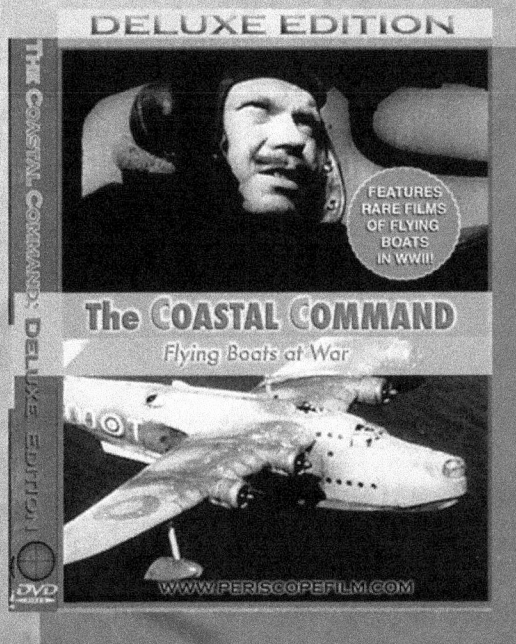

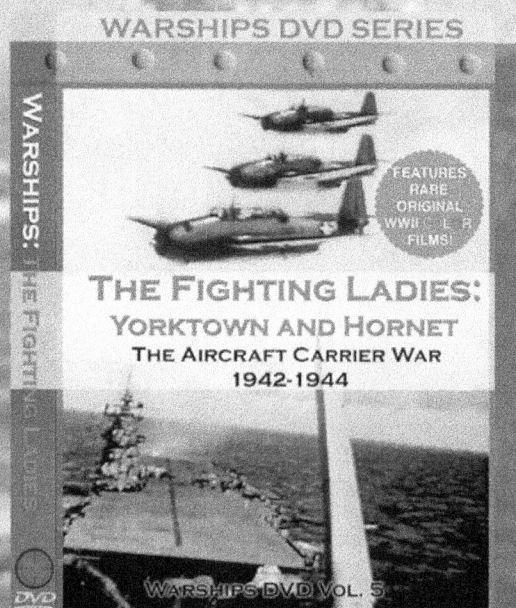

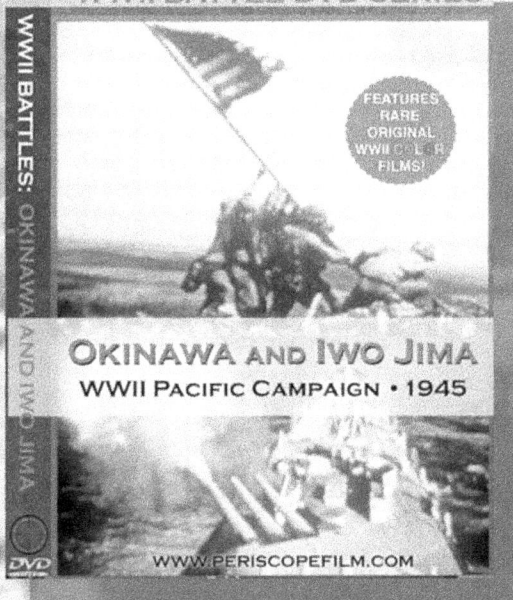

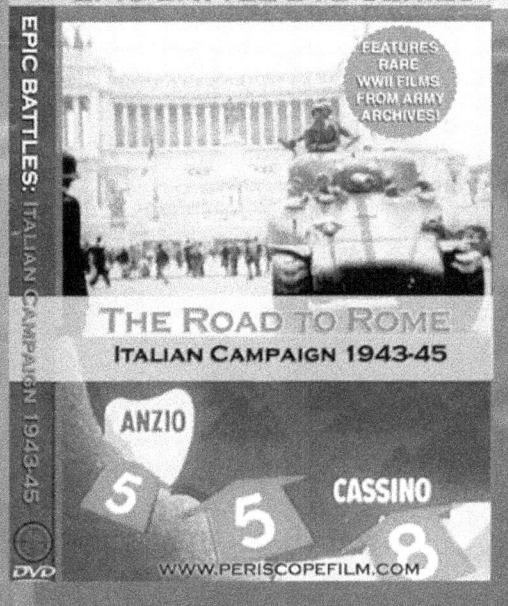

www.ingramcontent.com/pod-product-compliance
Lightning Source LLC
Chambersburg PA
CBHW081234090426
42738CB00016B/3308